Thinking Big Is Not Enough

Thinking Big Is Not Enough

Moving past the myths and misconceptions
that stop business growth

Michael G. Walsh

Book Cover Design: Trista Baldwin
Editor: Susan Kehoe
Assistant Editor: Nina Shoroplova
Production Editor: Jennifer Kaleta
Typeset: Greg Salisbury
Portrait Photographer: Kaizen Photography

This book is dedicated to my two children, Adam and Kathleen. To me, you both represent what's possible in the world. How exciting!

In Praise of Thinking Big
Is Not Enough

"*This is the most powerful, insightful, and practical book on how an entrepreneur can run a successful and profitable business. It demystifies why some businesses experience exponential growth while others struggle or fail. Michael passionately shares insights, strategies, and tools in a simple and engaging manner that will change your thinking and results forever.*"
Kim Deep, CPA, CMA, President, Business By Numbers Ltd.

"*Michael paints a descriptive, accurate picture of what is needed in balancing the allure of owning and growing a business with the challenges of making the vision a reality.*"
David Leeworthy, President, First Industries Corporation

"*Insightful, practical, relevant strategies that work right away, hit the core of the matter of business, and end in generating positive results - every single time. Michael, you are my secret weapon!*"
Azadeh Yaraghi, Creative Director/Owner, GOGO TELUGO Creatives

"*I am not a big book reader ... but when I opened the book, I was easily drawn to the story of Louise and the phenomenal growth she was able to achieve for her company through the help of Michael Walsh.*

"*The way the book is written allowed me to learn through Michael and Louise during the review of their journey. They served as my muse. I was able to see what worked and what did not work, as she grew her business. It was if I was given permission to be an invisible observer, allowed to see the inner details of the company without intruding.*

"*The summary of Myths and Perspective Shifts at the back of some of the chapters was a good focus for remembering the* key points of what I had read. The chapters on hiring were particularly beneficial. Wrong hiring choices over the years have cost me tens of thousands of dollars. Also extremely helpful were the 6 criteria points of A-Players, as well as the 10 attributes outside salespeople need to maximize success.

"The book has some wonderful takeaways and I was glad I took the time to read it cover to cover."
Barry Wood, Ernst and Young Entrepreneur of the Year

"This was a very engaging read. The format Michael has chosen to present his thoughts, ideas, and advice is reminiscent of The Wealthy Barber. It lays out fundamental ideas in an entertaining format while also presenting an inspirational story that is achievable by those willing to make fundamental change."
Jason Coolen, Physiotherapist, Clinic Director, PABC President

"We have worked with Michael Walsh in the past, and reading his book has been a great reminder of what we need to do on an ongoing basis to grow and stay successful.

"The tips given cut to the core of typical issues faced by business and go beyond the usual euphemisms and "top 10 lists" of how to improve your business. There is unique insight in regards to structure, with a healthy balance of risk versus reward. Some of the recommendations that we implemented following this guide have made a huge difference to our bottom line and as a business owner, my quality of life."
Kelly MacMillan, Managing Partner, MacMillan Team at Remax Elite

"Michael expertly removes many of the hurdles that limit the mindset of business owners and their perspective of how big and fast they can grow their business. I can't imagine a business owner who wouldn't benefit greatly from the lessons in this insightful book."
Mark Eiland, Founder and Principal Advisor, Mercury Equity Partners, Austin, Texas

"I've been experiencing a perspective shift recognizing that other small businesses are going through the same growing curve. We've been faced with all the myths and misconceptions in one form or another and it's been a great relief to see that there are solutions."
Bonnie Hood, Co-Founder, CMRev Fiber Optic Solutions

"I loved this book!! It's really down to earth, easy to read and easy to convert to action in my own business. It's a book that someone who is a budding business owner would find extremely valuable as well as a seasoned business owner. Our world is changing so rapidly and the concepts/matrix of this book provides any business owner with tools to support growth and profitability in all the changes we have now and are sure to have in the future. In every aspect the book teaches us about Partnership in all its forms. Effective partnership is the essence of success for the future of any business in our rapidly changing world."
Lucy Morris, President, Phoenix Possibilities Inc.

"Michael Walsh is one of my favourite entrepreneurial thinkers and I particularly love how his big thinking can wrap around all different kinds of businesses, including charities and social enterprises. His focus on our relationships and the opportunity for business building within a matrix of reciprocal and meaningful connections that allow us all to grow and thrive is invaluable. I look forward to sharing this new book with our colleagues, as much as I liked sharing his first book."
Aaron Johannes, M.A., Director, Spectrum Consulting- Collaborative Learning, Research and Press

"Michael Walsh helps create a business dream, and then describes the practical details on how to make that dream become reality. This is not a theoretical story, but an insider's sharing of the many considerations, steps and procedures in how a real business grew to great success. The content is not only the mechanics of business growth, but rare insight about how the business owner felt and needed to think about these transitions. The book is mostly a collection of easy to read stories, but do not let that fool you; the story is real and the experiences shared reflect on Michael's long history of bringing success to businesses."

Gary Braaksma, Founder, Braaksma Engineering

"I greatly enjoyed this case study on growing your business as presented through Michael's work with Louise Pasterfield and her experiences. This review clearly lays out the three core aspects of business growth in a simple, informative and entertaining style. Michael digs deep to explore the myths and misconceptions that Louise and many business owners often refer to that paralyses them from achieving their goals. I know I struggle with these clichés about business, and found myself relating with Louise on a number of them. Through Louise's point of view, Michael guides the reader through a process of critical thinking that result in eureka moments that he summarizes as 'Perspective Shifts.' *Thinking Big* is Not Enough outlines tools and criteria that will help many small business owners, who are passionate about what they do, take it to the next level."

Karen Marler, Princpal, Architect AIBC, AAA, SAA, OAA, FRAIC, LEED® AP

"This book was like reading about the last 3 years of our relationship—great job tying together all the business practices that you have shown me over those years. I want to go on your next trip to London."

Jim Allen, Founder and President, Jatec Electric Inc.

"Firstly let me say this book is very well written and easy to follow. As a long time client of yours I resonated with the process and the content and it brought me back to many parts of the growth journey that we have been on. It is a very concise manual on how to effectively grow a business and what is needed

But not only that—Michael has been able to convey this through a case study that allows you to see and understand the steps for yourself, rather than being told that this is how it works. I highly recommend this book to anyone who wants to achieve large scale growth without sacrificing customer service or burning yourself out."
Aldo Chies, Owner, A&B Tool Rentals Inc.

"In today's world where more, bigger, better is often thought as being the ultimate goal, Michael proves that Thinking Big is Not Enough. Using his practical and easy to read examples about how to marry together vision and structure to prepare and then carry out large scale growth—Michael takes the reader on the journey of his client, Louise, owner of Sponge UK and her exceptional growth; not just financial growth, but personal growth as well!"
Chantal Schutz, CA, Entrepreneur

"Since 2010 when we first started working with Michael Walsh, our company has grown consistently and most importantly with purpose. The insights that Michael brings, many of which are contained within this book, have given us the tools to grow, strengthen and shape our business consistent with our values. We are considerably stronger, more united and having a lot more fun."
Darryl Condon, Managing Principal, Hughes Condon Marler Architects

"Michael has a way of challenging you that initially catches you off guard but quickly leads to the heart of issues. Starting with the question of why we are doing something leads to terrific insights and shifted the way we looked at our business. I loved the notion of starting with where we want to be in 5 or 10 years and working backwards from there to see what we need to do this year."
Dave Ricketts | M.Sc., P.Eng., FEC, Managing Principal, Senior Building Science Specialist. RDH Building Engineering Ltd.

"When I first met Michael I was engaged by the way he could explain the challenges facing business owners, and the solutions required, in a straight forward manner. This continues in his book and it is invaluable for any business owner who is fed up with the headache that comes from hitting their head against the glass ceiling that prevents their business growth.

"For my part not only will I be using these ideas in my business, but my client's will also get to hear about them. Thanks Michael."
Paul Dodgshon, ACIB, Regional Partner, The Business, Partnership, Manchester, England

"Michael Walsh puts a context on how to approach business that is relevant, inspiring and applicable to how you live your life: work back from the big picture and stay in the present."
Dr. Manon Bolliger, ND, President, Cornerstone Health Centre and Bowen College

"Once again Michael has pulled the curtain back on our culture of entrepreneurial 'positive thinking' and tells the truth about what else it takes to successfully grow a business. He provides a straightforward account of the leadership and personal growth required by owners and the strategic viewpoints necessary to implement the operational strategies that support the vision for our companies. This book brought me right back into the room, as Louise navigated the various challenges of growth and departmental decisions she had to make as she came face to face with the misconceptions.

"If you are looking for the blueprint to successfully double or triple your business, this is for you."
Jolene McDonough, Founder, SYSTEMS SUCCESS, San Diego, California

"In pursuit of growing my small business I started working with Michael this year. Our sessions are always very intense and I leave them full of new knowledge and perspective on business.

to get there. *The story narrative is a nice way for the reader to relate to the journey and parts of it remind me of the style of* The E-Myth. *One of the strongest parts of the book for me was the way every chapter was concluded with a summary of myths, misconception and shifts in perspective. This is a fabulous way to capture all of the lessons in the chapter. I wish you much success with the book."*
Kevin Lang, President, Machine O Matic

"Michael's greatest strength is seeing from the outside the weaknesses and opportunities inside companies, their leaders and employees. His intuitive and knowledgeable guidance has helped countless businesses overcome their blockages and achieve previously unimaginable levels of growth.

"He brings tools to each business, no matter what type of business, that systemize, organize and most of all help strategize individuals and companies for future growth or continuous income.

"These tools are shared throughout this easy to read book through a real life example of one of his international clients. Step by step processes and myth busters create A-HA moments for the reader and opportunities to duplicate the success of the case study.

"If growing your business is what you are looking for, this book will open your eyes to new ways of thinking with real life processes. A must have for any entrepreneur, new or seasoned."
Doris Hager, President, Hager Design International Inc.

"This is not your typical business book. It provides insight into viewpoint changes necessary to help you grow your business, oriented around a detailed case study. I learned a lot!"
Diana Pederson, Co-Owner, NeuroKinetics Clinic

"This book gives access to the structure that is required to successfully and predictably achieve large scale growth in business,

The same is true of his book—it takes you on a journey and breaks down the misperceptions that hold us back from growth and excellence—with Louise as his muse, Michael shares his deep knowledge of the entrepreneur's journey and the fine balancing act it is to achieve significant growth and success in small - medium businesses."
Kelly Deck, Director, Kelly Deck Design

"I continue to be impressed with Michael's ability to describe a very large and complex process in a way that it is approachable, understandable and achievable. As a business owner, it is inspiring to know that the hard work, if done properly, can and will pay off. The tools described in Thinking Big is Not Enough are something we can all work with, in our own way, to make our businesses more than we have allowed ourselves to imagine."
Malcolm Cairns, Principal, Parallel Group Operations Inc.

"I was pleasantly surprised as to how incredibly easy it was to read and comprehend the essential elements of managing growth successfully. The book covers the obvious and not so obvious critical business dynamics from a practical viewpoint. I particularly appreciated the insights around hiring and developing key people."
David Malone, VP Business Initiatives, RBC Wealth Management

"As a small business owner, I found this book to have a profound impact on the way we are growing our organization. It was great to hear that we are not alone in our perceptions of growth, and the real-life break down of our common misconceptions was presented in an incredibly relatable fashion. In particular, I loved reading about the experience of expansion and development of the staff at Sponge UK and applying what they learned to my business.

"The description of the core functions of the staff, combined with detailing how to allow yourself permission to experiment and risk manage the investment of staffing growth, provides a unique understanding of when and how to add employees. The stories shared also provide clarity on how it is equally important to hire the right people, with defined lists of character traits to look for.

"I have never heard such comprehensive examples of using core values for building an effective and collaborative team. As our firm continues to grow, I will always turn back to this book as a reference for how someone else did it first, so I don't have to reinvent the wheel."

Marco A. Pugliese, Co-Founder, Sales and Marketing, One Smart Home, Edmonton, Alberta, Canada

"Overall, I found the book to be a very accurate portrayal of the experiences that I have had in building my own company. Having worked closely with Michael Walsh & Kaizen Consulting, I found it interesting to see the concepts we have been working with for several years presented in this book. While no single text can be a complete resource, I am incredibly impressed with this collection of business practices. A reader can expect to achieve piercing insight into his own operation while reading about Sponge UK ... and new insights each time the book is read. I feel inspired to apply what I learned to my own operation immediately."

Mike Burris, Co-Founder, Operations, One Smart Home, Edmonton, Alberta, Canada

"Having met Michael and a number of characters in the book, what appears to translate so well, is the energy. I know how the process has begun to assist us and can see how the book will begin to help others. The narrative tone makes this an enjoyable and easy read ... "

Nick Palfrey, CEO, Real Visual Group, Plymouth, UK

"*True to form, in telling a story, Michael effectively dispels the myths and misconceptions that prevent businesses from growing and offers very compelling arguments for making shifts in one's perspective on what really matters to grow a business. In the process he successfully points the reader to focusing on the key essentials for achieving 'large scale growth.'*"

Philippe de Clerck, MPT, MBA, VP Operations, and Partner, Back in Motion Rehab Inc.

"*This book is fresh and attractive as it conveys a genuine live experience in the light of friendship and success. It brings to the surface lots of experiential information taking advantage in the process of resolving a thread of intricate paradoxes one after the other using a very thought provoking but also gentle and intimate human angle of approach.*

"*This book is the definite pre-take-off check list for success to tackle both definite and not well resolved directional and topical issues in all kinds of business operations.*"

Philippe A. Souvestre, M.D., DESS, CES, CEA/PhD,
Neurosciences (France), Traumatology, Aerospace Medicine, Sports Medicine. R.R.P. (Canada), R.Ac. (BC), President and Director of Programs, NeuroKinetics Health Services (B.C.), Inc.

"*I read this book very quickly and genuinely enjoyed the experience. The dialogue kept me thinking 'big picture,' and prevented me from looking for a formula that would never apply. It was the very book I should have read five years ago as it would have made a big difference on certain decisions.*

"*For entrepreneurs, seeing the future and visualizing the trajectory of our business over a long period of time is hard because we are so caught up in the here and now of getting our venture off the ground. That focus is essential but it is also deadly because we forget to step back. We need more books like this that help us get our nose out of our business so we can see where we*

need to go next. I love that I didn't come away with a 'how to' for my own ventures and instead came away with a 'why not?'!"
Mr. Shannon Stange, Entrepreneur, Vancouver, BC

"Due to a very busy schedule, this book is the only one I have read in the past 6 months. I am glad that I did though. I have worked with over 800 small business owners during the past 5 years. It is clear that Michael understands the challenges of running and growing a small business. This book will provide business owners with the knowledge needed to avoid the potholes on the route to business success, by taking them down a road they probably, at this point in time, didn't know existed. Powerful ideas, clearly articulated and supported by a real life example are a recipe for helping business owners move further, faster. It is a wonderful demonstration of what can be achieved if business owners are open to learning and growing."
Steven Edwards, Leadership and Management Specialist, Growth Accelerator, Business Growth Service, UK

"Michael Walsh has such a thorough knowledge and experience around business management, growth and development, which he shares in this book. Thinking Big is Not Enough is a business owner's handbook, a guide to not only navigate the challenges but to take your business to the next level. I find Michael's approach and the information in this book to be immensely helpful, reassuring and inspirational."
Emma Richmond, Co-Founder, Co-Owner, The Sound Experience Inc.

"Michael Walsh provides a fresh perspective on the challenges to growth faced by business owners today. His approach is different than typical business self help books and provides new solutions to overcome many of the common business myths. Having engaged Michael's services for my own business, I can attest to the validity of his methods. Business and its challenges evolve, the solutions should too. Thinking Big is Not Enough: to Moving

past the myths, and misconceptions that stop business growth *will enlighten business owners to lead that evolution."*
William F. Jones, Jr., CPA, Partner | Anton Collins Mitchell LLP, Boulder, Colorado

"The graphic of the spinning plates on the foundation resting on a ball was a real 'a-ha', in fact, I laughed out loud and thought I'd better print it and stick it somewhere I can see it daily. It made me feel a lot better, realizing the enormous complexity and challenge in running and growing a business; sometimes I feel I should just be able to do this as if it were a 'job' and easily. I forget that a business is comprised of a dozen different 'jobs' or more and if I'm doing all of them and making a profit, then that is a big win and needs to be acknowledged. 'To achieve success in business, it really is more about shifting a large number of little things in a variety of different areas that add up to making a big collective difference.' This was really good for me too. Putting a little more spin on each plate day by day, as it were, will get the job done more effectively and faster than 'slogging' it out."
Katherine Lazaruk, AICI FLC, ICU Image Consulting, Inc.

Acknowledgements

For a long time, I thought the act of writing was a solitary act. Eventually, I realized that this is so narrow in thinking that it is simply inaccurate. I see more and more that it is a creative and combined community effort. It is only with and through a community that anything of substance gets written. While the writing itself may not be a group exercise, the writing itself is only part of any creative work. This book has been no exception.

Mr. Shannon Stange, thank you for your efforts in facilitating a strong writing community with the Just Write Vancouver Meetup. Thank you too, for the recommendation to Julie Salisbury, an extraordinary publisher and guide.

Julie Salisbury of Influence Publishing, you have opened my eyes on what it takes to write and deliver a project such as this all along the way. I have been learning constantly from you. Thank you to you and your team, who have provided effective direction and support in so many ways to this project.

Sue Kehoe, who helped craft raw dialogue and well-intended ideas into a cogent presentation—you are an amazing gift. Thank you.

Cara Bedford, I am still learning social media. You and your team are making that easier for me to share ideas with others. Thanks!

Steve Moxness, when a hurricane and a competing project both threatened the progress on this book, you really came through for me. I appreciate your innovation, your generosity, and your friendship.

To the think-tank with whom I have the privilege of working with each day, testing and evaluating ideas for the benefit of our clients—George Opsahl, Allan Newbury, Loris Martin, Chuck Scharenberg, Don Brewster, Norm Duplessis and Cathy Nurmi—thanks for your ongoing ideas, questions, brainstorming, and participation in support of our respective and collective clients.

To a special group of about 50 clients, colleagues, and friends, thank you for providing effective and encouraging feedback on this book and the ideas it contains along the way. You know who you are. I appreciate each of you.

To John Warrillow—thanks for the inspiration your first book provided, and for that entrepreneurial spirit you bring to everything you do. We all win due to your contributions to business growth and value.

To the community of Value Builders—thanks for the feedback and the encouragement. I am honoured to be part of this community.

Lucy Morris, the journey continues to unfold. Thanks for your part in keeping me sane and grounded through all this. Your contributions are immeasurable.

To the many clients from whom I have learned so many things over these past two decades about what it takes to grow and sustain an increasingly profitable enterprise, you are the reason I do this. I learn from you every day. Thank you for your openness to the ideas of others, and your willingness to play fully in building your businesses.

To the people at Sponge UK, your commitment to growth and contribution is clear every time I work with any one of you. I appreciate the opportunity to play as part of your team, from "across the pond."

Louise Pasterfield, it continues to be an honour and a privilege to work with you. Thank you for opening up your business to the outsider's view, sharing so powerfully your story and what you have learned. I look forward to continuing to assist you as you unfold the next chapters of your growth and evolution.

Most important of all, to Grace: without your wisdom, your patience and your tireless support, there is no way this book would have ever been done. On this I am clear. Words cannot describe the depth of love and appreciation I have for you. Thank you for your partnership in life.

Contents

Foreword

Grade school economics teaches us that companies grow in a predictable trajectory from start-up to growth to maturity.

In real life, I have found business growth to be somewhat less predictable.

Most days, I feel like I'm running on a treadmill—working as hard as I can just to stay in one place. It's not until I pull back the aperture of the lens that I can see we're making a little progress here and there.

But it's still not linear.

In fact, I think a more accurate visual of the business lifecycle is a series of plateaus that require a spastic leap to get to the next one. Sometimes you cross the void and find yourself neatly perched on the next level; other times you have one foot on the plateau and another dangling in the air as you try and muster the courage to make the next leap.

The first plateau involves figuring out something customers want to buy. You can stay at this plateau for years, experimenting with different products and services until something finally sticks.

Next is the task of learning how to consistently deliver the product or service customers are willing to pay for. Again, many businesses stay stuck at this phase for years or decades, just trying to develop a repeatable formula for satisfying customers.

The next plateau involves a giant leap to a business that can hire and train employees to consistently do the work with as much passion as the owner brings to their job.

The hallmark of the plateau model is that once you have arrived at a new level, you're not at much risk of falling backwards, but there is also a big leap required to get to the next stage, and the length of time you stall at a specific step can be months or years.

In Thinking Big Is Not Enough, Michael Walsh illustrates how to push through the obstacles that stand between you and the next plateau quickly and consistently.

Michael will introduce you to a woman named Louise Pasterfield who runs a business in England. You may ask yourself what on earth you can learn from a British woman operating in an unrelated industry. But read on and I think you'll find that Louise's story is eerily similar to a lot of businesses. It may even have something in common with yours: a non-linear path to success that looks more like a series of stepping stones than the graph we learned at school.

Michael is a master storyteller; enjoy the journey he takes you on.

John Warrillow

Founder of The Value Builder System™ and author of *Built to Sell: Creating A Business That Can Thrive Without You* and *The Automatic Customer: Creating a Subscription Business in Any Industry.*

INTRODUCTION

How do you grow a business? I mean, really grow it much bigger than it already is. This is a question that plagues many business owners—large and small.

There are many business consultants and coaches who will tell you how to do it, and while many of them share some ideas, no two strategies are the same. That's because there are many ways to grow a business.

There are also many ways to get stuck. The real gold is not in talking about how to grow. It lies in determining where we get stuck, and keeping ourselves free of these traps.

Many of the traps we fall into lie in the thinking about what it takes to grow a business. There is a great deal of conventional wisdom on how to do that. Much of this "wisdom" is flawed. So that leaves us with the question, *how do you sort out good thinking from bad when growing a business?*

The answer is simple. You check with people who have done it. They have travelled down the path of growth, and they have found a way to get past those traps.

This book was designed to give you a glimpse into the journey of one such business owner, midstream through the growth process.

Louise Pasterfield, Managing Director of Sponge UK, has been actively at work growing her already established company for the past three years. So far, she has achieved a five-fold increase in gross revenues, with a commensurate increase in net income as well.

As she plans the next five-fold increase of her business, we look back at her progress over the past three years: what she has done, where the traps were, and what she discovered along the way.

This book is presented as a story, though the story is real. The only names that were changed were those of three people she had to let go along the way. After clarifying why "thinking big is not enough" in Chapter 1, and setting the stage by introducing Louise and how we met in Chapter 2, Chapters 3 through 13 recount the review she and I conducted of her journey growing her business over these past three years.

Rather than setting a structured (read: textbook) format, I have chosen to let it flow, just as the conversation did when Louise and I did our three-year review in June 2014. We discuss the obstacles she faced (myths and misconceptions), shifts in her perspective, and introduce helpful tools as we explore her experience growing her company to the next level.

After the review in Chapters 3 through 13, we shift gears in Chapter 14 and identify what Louise needs to work on next to maintain the momentum she has gained, and to take her business to yet another level of growth.

In the Afterword, I challenge you to change the way you think about how to grow your business. I challenge you to start asking questions, many of them, rather than simply looking for quick answers. This too is a perspective shift and a necessary one if you want to be successful in taking your business to the next level. There are many areas that need to be addressed when growing a business. Asking the right questions is the key. I also provide you with access to additional free resources for business growth available directly through our website at Kaizen Consulting. *Thinking big is not enough!*

I hope you enjoy the journey.

Michael Walsh
Kaizen Consulting Services Inc.

1 Why Thinking Big Is Not Enough

"You never become a howling success by just howling."
Bob Harrington, Reverend and Motivational Speaker

We love thinking big.

It is very exciting! Entrepreneurs dream of a future that is brighter, and then we go and make it happen.

Business has the power to transform lives. We go into business with the idea of making a difference for others and for ourselves. We want to feel satisfaction, self-expression, and to contribute to the people around us. We want to build something that makes us proud.

Most of all, we want freedom.

We want the freedom to create, the freedom to choose, the freedom to engage with life on our own terms. We know that to get more freedom, we had better design and operate our business more effectively, with more profit.

More profit means more freedom. That's what we want, and to do that we need to get bigger.

We have all had a job before getting into our own businesses, and we have felt the constraints that are present in working for others—living life on their terms. There's definitely not much freedom in that.

We dream about a better life, and we set out to do something about it. We either build from scratch, or we buy into a business, then we're ready to go.

We hear of stories of entrepreneurs who make it big. Whether it is Steve Jobs and Steve Wozniak, or Bill Gates and Paul Allen, or Sir Richard Branson, we see these larger-than-life characters and we go for it.

The energy of thinking big is very alluring. Whether it is a big business—Apple, Microsoft, Virgin—or a big idea—stop global warming, eradicate oppression, save the world—we know that business is where we can make things happen. In business, we have the freedom to create whatever we can dream.

We each have our own version of thinking big. Another term for that is Vision.

VISION

Vision has very fast energy. This is our passion, our inspiration, our intuitive sense, our purpose in business and in life.

This is the energy of thinking big.

Any of the 20+ million people who have seen the video of Simon Sinek's 2009 TED Talk, *How Great Leaders Inspire Action*, have watched Sinek describe a simple model for clarifying our Vision, followed by three compelling examples of inspirational leadership in action. His message is simple: People do not buy what you do; they buy WHY you do it. We see this video and become inspired to start looking for and sharing our "Why"— the core reason for our existence. Vision is powerful. I have seen that video a number of times, and each time it reaches into me and sets my passion burning.

Yes, with Vision, we can make things happen.

It is no wonder that we migrate to the notion of thinking big. With all the passion that gets unleashed, we can make lots happen, very quickly.

What is it about Vision that ignites our passions?

Vision = Limbic Energy

The circulation system in the body is a closed system. Our blood flows within us, but not beyond us (at least not if we are healthy!). If I met you for a coffee, and if I had some sort of blood disorder (thankfully, I don't), you couldn't catch the disorder by sitting across from me at a table. That is because my circulatory system is a closed system. Yours is too.

The limbic system, on the other hand, is an open system. If you walked into a room full of friends and colleagues who were laughing and joking around, you may soon find yourself laughing as well. Or if they were very somber and sad, you might find your mood growing darker. Both good and bad moods can be contagious.

The limbic system is tied directly to our emotions. Unlike the circulatory system, the limbic system is open and subject to the influence of others.

That's what makes powerful leadership so inspiring. A compelling leader can influence us by tapping into our emotions. We get excited very quickly.

Notice that we don't even have to be in the same room as the other person to have our emotions tapped. We can see a video (like a motivational TED talk), read a book, or watch a great movie.

A really good movie is one that takes us on an emotional journey. If the film-makers have done their job well, we may laugh at times, we may cry at others, and we will be holding our breath at suspenseful moments. This is limbic energy in action.

Since our emotions can be fired up so quickly, when we think big thoughts for our business, it gives us access to that limbic energy—that passion, that inspiration, that intuition, and that purpose. That's what allows the energy of Vision to move so incredibly fast. The energy of Vision has us feeling like anything is possible!

Yet, no matter how alluring Vision is, it is only half of the story. Without Structure to support our Vision, either chaos is created or our vision falls flat.

Vision without Structure creates chaos or it falls flat.

STRUCTURE

Structure is the other side of the equation. Where Vision has very fast energy, Structure has very slow, stable energy. Where Vision is the energy of emotion, Structure is the energy of logic.

Within our businesses, Structure may take on many forms. Our processes, our systems, our procedures, our methods, and the supports that back us up are all structural forms of energy. Structures form the underpinnings of our businesses, without which, our Visions would be worthless.

That said; Structure without Vision is like slogging through the mud. It is very constraining and not much fun.

Structure without Vision is like slogging through the mud.

Yet, when we come under attack in our business or face major adversity, many of us dump Vision and head into what appears to be the safe protection of Structure.

Then we wonder why business just got so much harder!

To be effective in business, we need both Vision and Structure working for us consistently. Both emotion and logic. Vision is the easy, intuitive part. The hard part, requiring conscious thought and discipline, is Structure.

THE CHALLENGE OF GROWING A BUSINESS

Owning, operating, and growing a business presents big challenges. Unfortunately, many of us have trouble tapping the riches that lie within our companies to achieve that growth.

Why is that?

The reason is that multiple things are going on at any given time and we aren't always prepared or positioned to deal with them all. Sometimes we need to address only a few of them; sometimes we need to address all of them at once.

To understand this more fully, let's explore this in more depth.

RUNNING A BUSINESS IS A BALANCING ACT

When we work for someone else, we produce and deliver products and services for the company in which we work. Our job involves juggling a number of variables in the process of producing and delivering those products—a balancing act.

Imagine I am an architect. There are a great number of complexities in this role. As an architect, I would have multiple variables to deal with in delivering my craft to the company's clients where I work.

There are the elements of building design, city zoning requirements, and the building code for whatever municipality will host the new building. Then there is the task of integrating my design with the work of the consulting engineers and other specialists involved in the design process. Once working drawings are completed, submitted to the municipality, and approved, there is the process of tendering the work to contractors, one of whom will build the building that has been designed. Oversight is then needed, to ensure that what was designed is what gets built.

It could be said that this is like a plate spinning on a stick. Many different variables need to be addressed to be successful within this or any complex profession (see Figure 1.1).

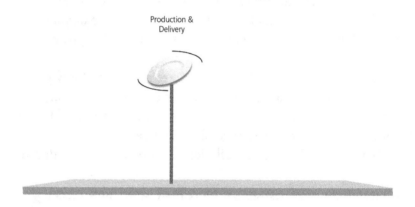

Production &
Delivery

Figure 1.1 - A spinning plate on a stick, balanced on a foundation of knowledge and skills—the task of anyone with a complex profession or job. Deliver something of value either to or on behalf of the Boss.

However, when running a business, there is much more occurring than just getting the job done.

1. There is the process of finding and enticing customers to buy from us—to use our company to fill their need for products or services (Sales and Marketing).

2. Then there is the process of providing a product or service, and delivering it as promised. This is the foundation of many small to medium-sized businesses. We learned how to provide a product or service while working for someone else. Then, at some point, we decided to step out on our own, either alone or with others, to try our hand at doing this independently (Production and Delivery).

3. Of course, we can't forget the process of dealing with the fiscal aspects of the business. This involves everything from pricing high enough to make money, yet low enough to keep our customers coming back; to setting terms for collection; to tracking our cash flows in order to keep us funded well enough to meet payroll, while keeping our suppliers happy; to covering our government remittances and having something left over for ourselves (The Money).

4. In addition, there is the human resources component to this ... our staff members. For many of us, this is the trickiest part of all. This includes everything from hiring the right people for us, to getting them trained and up to speed, and getting them to do what we need them to do when we need it done. There is also the task of keeping them happy, so that after all that work of finding and training them, they don't just leave and go to work for our competitor (The People).

Regardless of how complicated the core product or service is, running a business that delivers that product or service is even more challenging, as illustrated in Figure 1.2.

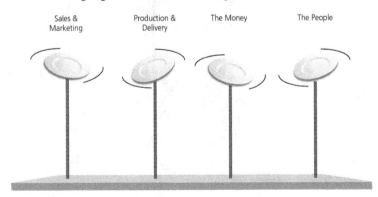

Figure 1.2 - Four spinning plates on sticks, balanced on our foundation. This gets closer to what it takes to deal with the different aspects of running a business.

As an architect, I conceptualize, design, coordinate, draw, approve, submit, oversee, and more until the building is finally completed. Then my job is done and we hope the building will stand for fifty years or more.

This is simply not the case with a business. In addition to those four plates spinning, there is another variable at play.

5. As business owners, we operate in a constantly shifting marketplace, where technological advances, evolving ways in how our customers access products and services, and new ways of attracting and doing business keep many aspects of our business shifting in ways we rarely anticipate. This is like constructing a building on ground that keeps shifting even after we have finished construction. The job is never done (The Marketplace).

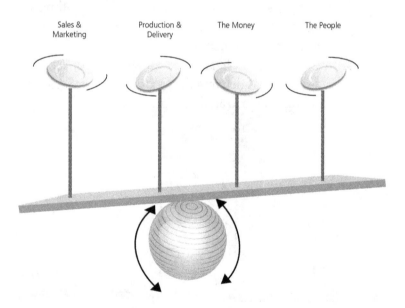

Figure 1.3 - Four spinning plates on sticks, balanced on our foundation that is teetering on a ball that moves. Now THIS is what it is like to operate a business in the constantly shifing dynamics of the marketplace.

This is closer to what it is really like to operate a business!

Yes, finding and maintaining that ongoing balance among all these constantly shifting parameters is quite a challenge.

It is this complexity within a constantly changing environment that is the dynamic that makes starting, operating, and growing a business challenging.

If I were that architect, my studies would not have prepared me for what it takes to run and grow an architectural business. The architectural school's mandate is to teach me how to become a solid architect, informed in the ways of architecture, not business.

Business schools help us learn the general principles of business. However, they usually focus on how to think about business, and on big business models, not small to medium enterprises. Public companies have data readily available. Private companies don't. Further, the best business schools provide us with generalities and principles, not the nuances that we will have to learn and use in our industry and with the regional differences we each face.

No, there really is no place to go to get a practical education about growing a business ... other than the marketplace itself.

Some people get into business with the support and guidance of a mentor, such as with a business that is passed down from a parent to a child. Others need to fend for themselves and figure it out along the way.

Despite the challenges of starting a business, many of us actually find a way to operate and grow a business to a certain level. We find a way to strike a balance among all the competing elements involved in operating a profitable enterprise. However, it is not unusual to see business owners settle in at certain levels of sales—plateaus—past which they find it hard to scale.

That plateau could be at half a million in sales per year, it might be at one million or two million per year. For other companies the plateau might even be at ten million or more in annual sales. Most of us hit one of these plateaus at some point, and then we seem to get stuck there.

We soon discover that if we want to grow beyond that level—beyond the plateau—the previous balance we had achieved and felt comfortable with pretty much goes out the window!

GROWING A BUSINESS IS AN ART

After overcoming all the hurdles to establish a viable, functioning company, we push for growth. There are a number of factors that may be driving us to grow:

- We have reached a plateau and want to move beyond it.
- One or more of the elements of our current business is out of balance and we hope that growth will help us get it back.
- We are doing so at the insistence of our key customers. If we can't handle their evolving needs, they will be forced to take their business elsewhere.
- We are doing so for our own hunger for what is available at new and higher levels. Thinking big is very alluring.
- We haven't yet reached our goals. We have further to go, to get what we want.

So we grow.

And when we grow, many of the norms we have established and the rules we have set for ourselves for balancing the competing priorities no longer apply. Most of what we learned to hit the balance point at our current level stops working when we try to move to that next level. We need to find the new balance point. We need to find new ways of doing things and a new perspective.

The Good News: More Businesses Survive!

We've all heard that most businesses don't survive past the first five years. The most common statistic that was being thrown around twenty years ago was that only 15 percent of all new businesses were still operating five years after inception.

According to government statistics, more businesses are succeeding now than ever before. The number of businesses that survive beyond the first five years has grown to around 45 percent on average.[1] That is a significant change and worth celebrating.

Growth Can Be Tricky

Yet large-scale business growth is another matter. Based on data extrapolated from information available through the US Small Business Administration Advocacy and the 2011 US Census:

- Eighty-five percent of all businesses within the United States never reach $1 million in sales.
- Of those that do reach the $1 million mark, 95 percent of them never hit $5 million.
- Of those companies that achieve $5 million in sales, 98 percent of these companies never reach $10 million in annual revenues.

The numbers are similar in other countries throughout the world. While business survival is on the upswing, the odds of significant business growth are still very slim.

There is no doubt about it. Growing a business is tricky.

Imagine spinning all those plates, balancing on the ever-shifting market conditions, all while trying to add more plates and trying to move forward!

That's why it can be a handful. However ...

---

[1]United States Small Business Profile, U.S. Small Business Administration, Office of Advocacy, 2014.

GROWTH IS POSSIBLE!

Although the number of businesses that grow to become large companies is relatively small, it does happen. We do hear of the success stories; some people do succeed in achieving large-scale growth for their businesses. Remember, every big business was small once. For optimists like us, that is good news. As entrepreneurs, we are used to going up against such odds.

If we can understand and overcome the obstacles that stop us from achieving our goals for growth, maybe we *can* get what we want from our businesses after all!

In order to overcome these obstacles, we need to be aware of the many myths and misconceptions about scaling a business out there in the business world. These well-intentioned, albeit misguided, notions actually get in our way rather than help us.

It is only by sorting fact from fiction that we may scale the hurdles to growth and achieve the goals we set for our businesses and ourselves.

While each of us will find our own path, adopting good strategies and avoiding the well-intentioned bad advice that is out there is essential.

In this book, we explore the experiences of one entrepreneur as she and I review her three-year journey along the path to large-scale business growth and development for herself, her staff, and her company.

Louise Pasterfield, an ambitious woman from Plymouth, England and creator of an enterprising elearning company called Sponge UK has started to figure out fact from fiction.

She shares her story with us: the obstacles she faced, discoveries she made, shifts in her perspective as she grew, and many of the specific tips and tools she has acquired and is using in support of her quest for growth, profit, and freedom.

Now, let's go to England!

2 To England!

"A ship is safe in harbor, but that's not what ships are for."
John A. Shedd, Salt from My Attic, 1928.

As the Heathrow Express pulled into London's Paddington Train Station this past summer, I recalled the first time I had travelled here from my home in Vancouver, Canada, three years earlier. I wasn't quite sure what to expect on that, my first visit to the UK.

I had only been to Europe once, ten years before that, and never to England. The train system certainly seemed efficient and comfortable and a great alternative to trying to navigate my way in a car down the left side of the roads in this country.

There was so much that was different about England: the architecture, the culture, people's accents, the driving.

Would business be different here too?

I have started, grown, and sold businesses in Toronto, Canada. Then for the past two decades, I have supported clients throughout North America from my business consulting firm based in Vancouver and Chicago. Over the years, I have found that despite cultural and geographical differences, as well as varying economic conditions, people in business seem to have similar goals, concerns, opportunities, issues, and challenges.

I expected, and counted on the fundamentals being the same in Europe as well. In hindsight, while there were a few differences—like employee-to-sales ratios with different currencies—most of what I have encountered over the past three years has been no more different between North America and Europe than the variances between differing industries within the same economy.

All businesses have one thing in common. They are all owned, operated, and staffed by people, in service of their customers and clients, who are also people.

MEET LOUISE PASTERFIELD

Louise Pasterfield owns a company, Sponge UK, that was originally a spin-out company of Gusto Creative, a small design and marketing agency that Louise and her husband Mark had owned and operated for some time. In 2003, Mark was no longer active in the business due to an ongoing health problem. Louise found herself running the company with her adult daughter, Kate, and about six staff. Revenues in Gusto Creative had settled in at £250,000 per annum. (For those unfamiliar with the British Pound, £1 has been roughly equivalent to $1.60 US dollars over the past ten years.)

After winning a large learning contract from the government, Louise became interested in online learning. She had become bored with design in marketing. After doing that for twenty years, it no longer got her excited. She began exploring online learning opportunities, meeting with a number of elearning experts. It gave her the idea to start Sponge a year later, in 2004. Sponge was launched as a company to provide bespoke elearning solutions (online learning modules) for its clients. All of the staff underwent training in elearning software, and the company continued to gain ground.

Then in 2010, the worldwide financial collapse caught up with Sponge. Despite Sponge having a relatively strong year (about £400,000 per annum in revenues with ten staff that included Louise and her daughter, Kate), the bank cut their overdraft line of credit in half, due to the prolonged recession.

Louise always thought Sponge had huge potential, and she really wanted to grow the business. That's when she started to look for books and articles online about how to grow a business.

FIRST CONTACT

When I think back to how I first connected with Louise, I remember that it almost didn't happen, except for her persistence. Out of the blue, I received an email from a woman in England, of all places. This woman was asking for help with the growth of her small business.

I have periodically received requests and email inquiries from people from countries outside Canada or the US, but usually they had been from people who were interested in either taking our Consultant Training, or others who wanted jobs in consulting. We seemed to get inquiries about once per month from people on different continents. Back in 2011, we were not set up to support or collaborate with people outside of North America.

Treating this email from England as being of the same nature, I briefly considered it and then promptly forgot about it.

However, a week later, I received a follow-up email from Louise. "I'm not sure if you received my previous correspondence from last week, so I thought I would write to you again ... Might we set up a WebEx call?"

Based on this woman's persistence, and feeling a little

sheepish for ignoring her earlier request, I replied and we set up the call. Louise and Kate had a full presentation ready for me in PowerPoint, sharing the company's financial history, a background on their services—developing elearning modules for other companies throughout Europe—as well as their hopes for the future and the challenges they faced.

When I asked Louise how she found me, she explained, "I came across some of the articles which you had written, and they intrigued me. They weren't the usual old regurgitated stuff I often find online. It was clear you understood the challenges of owning a small business, and wanting to be bigger. So I ordered and read your book, which impressed me further.[2]

"I found it unusual and refreshing. One of the things you said, for example, was that to achieve large-scale growth in your business, you had to have a fundamental respect for people. That was one of the items listed in your criteria to scale a company—very unusual for a consultant to say, but it makes total sense.

"I also liked your insistence in taking enough time off and having regular breaks and holidays, not as a reward, but as a requirement to properly grow the business. That was refreshing to hear!

"Working my way through the book, I became more convinced that it really was possible to grow the business, but I knew I would need some help. At the end of the book was an invitation to contact you, so I did, and here we are."

MY FIRST IMPRESSIONS

Other than potential geographic and logistical challenges, everything Louise and Kate expressed on that WebEx call was

---

[2]Walsh, Michael G. *Business Growth by Design: A Business Owner's Guide To Tapping Your Potential Without Getting Tapped Out.* Vancouver, BC: Kaizen Consulting Services Inc. 2010.

similar to many of the smaller clients we have assisted in their efforts to grow and prosper.

Louise, age fifty-two at the time, had lots of heart and plenty of smarts, as well as a well-established working business, but she didn't quite know how to take it to the next level of growth.

At that time, I was working almost exclusively either live one-to-one with business owners and their key staff, or with a combination of live work and consistent telephone support between visits. The hurdle of a nine-hour overseas flight with an eight-hour time difference still lay in our path, blocking any potential to work together.

However, one of our core values at Kaizen is "Dare to venture." I figured, nothing ventured, nothing gained.

So I said to Louise, "Well, I have never been to England before. If you cover expenses, I will waive my fees for this visit, and I will come over and invest a few days in assisting you in the growth of your business. We can treat it like a test-drive of a potential working arrangement. My promise to you is that you will gain value well in excess of your time and expense reimbursement investment. From my side, I can always combine it with a holiday over there, so we can both win, regardless of what the future holds."

I knew I could help Louise out during our planned few days together. However, neither she nor I had any idea what a working relationship might look like if we decided there was good synergy between us. The only real question left for me was whether we could work well together. For that, I would want to meet her team and get a feel for how she operates with her people. That would tell me what I needed to know about whether she could work with me, and vice versa. We invest far too much time working directly with clients to enter into arrangements before we know that we will work well together.

I had done these types of "test-drive" trips before, usually for one to two days, and always within North America. In those cases, if the fit was right, I could see the potential of working together since travel was far less of an issue when staying on the same continent.

Despite the uncertainty of what might follow, the arrangement sounded reasonable to Louise as well, so she agreed and we set up plans for my trip to England.

PADDINGTON TRAIN STATION - JUNE 2011

I met Louise in person for the first time on the platform at London's Paddington Train Station in June 2011.

I had taken the Heathrow Express to Paddington, with my luggage in tow, including my banjo, neatly tucked in its case. I had recently taken up this instrument, and I discovered that if I didn't keep practicing daily—even during travel—any gains would quickly be lost. I figured I would have time to practice in the evenings. I have found this to be a valuable method to settle down and relax after a long day of client meetings.

As I approached the end of the platform after leaving the shuttle train, I saw a sophisticated looking woman clutching something in her hand and scanning the crowd expectantly. Drawing closer, I recognized the item she held … my book! It was then that I knew that this was the person who was there to greet me, accompany me on the three-and-a-half hour commute by rail to the Southwest English town of Plymouth, and with whom I would be working over the next several days.

All I had known about Plymouth before this trip was that it was the place in England from where the pilgrims first sailed to America aboard the *Mayflower*.

"I didn't know if I would recognize you from this little picture," Louise said with a triumphant grin, while holding up the book. She did a bit of a double take at the banjo case and asked me about it. After I filled her in, she let it drop, but only after looking at it inquisitively.

We started the process of getting to know each other over a quick bite of lunch. Then at my prompting, Louise gave me a bit more background on herself. She was originally born in the United States, and moved to the UK to go to university. That was when she met Mark, to whom she has been married for over three decades.

Mark and Louise have three children, all girls. In addition to Kate, there is also Laura and Nicola, each in their twenties at that time. I could tell by meeting her that Louise was, above all else, a mother. She was committed to the care of those around her. She made sure that I was properly acclimated to my new surroundings.

After lunch we boarded the train to Plymouth and we were on our way.

Within five minutes of the train's departure, I started.

"Are you ready to begin?" I asked.

Louise was a bit surprised by this, but happily agreed.

I guess she expected me to nod off on the trip to Plymouth, which I eventually did toward the end of our train ride, but not until I had her participate in a couple of key exercises, and after I got to know her a bit better.

I was not aware that this train ride, exercises, and polite conversation would be the start of a major growth campaign by a woman with a quiet drive and determination that was exceeded only by her positive spirit and supportive nature.

THREE YEARS LATER: BACK IN THE UK

Fast-forward to June 2014. I'm back in the UK, for my fourth trip since we started. We are beginning our review of the past three years of working together: noticing what levels of growth have been achieved, the changes in the staff, and the growth of the company in general.

With a current staff of twenty-nine people, Louise knows that the company will generate £2,000,000 in revenues this calendar year, which represents a five-fold growth from four years ago, the year before we started working together. She was really hoping to push sales to £2,400,000 to achieve a six-fold increase within that four-year period, but she knows that would have been a stretch with current staffing levels.

More important than that, Louise says that she is having the time of her life. She has never had as much fun in business. She is constantly learning new things. She is dealing with more substantive challenges than ever before, and she is really excited about the future.

The company's net income this year will far exceed her gross revenues from four years ago. With the help of Matt, the company's part-time CFO (Chief Financial Officer), Sponge has been growing its financial reserves. This is good, since Louise wants to reinvest by adding significantly to her staff and adding other resources to take her company to a new level.

In fact, what this current visit to the UK is about is to support Louise in setting up the company to take the leap from her current level of £2 million per annum to £10+ million, a goal she is certain is achievable within the next three to four years. Then, she wants to grow it to £20 million and beyond—a seven-year goal—before stepping down and handing the reigns to someone else.

"You know, Michael," said Louise, "even though we initially started three years ago by talking about growing a much larger company, I didn't really believe it was actually achievable at this level. I knew that theoretically it was possible, and I thought it would be great if I got there, but I didn't get it at the time."

"Not that I told you that," she added with a smirk.

Louise continued.

"My real goal—the one I thought I could achieve—was to build the company up to £1 million per year in sales. Yet, you could see so much more, so clearly.

"Don't get me wrong," she added. "I wanted everything we have planned and achieved. I was just surprised that I didn't see it before."

"So Louise," I asked, "what changed that allowed you and your team to generate these results in your business?"

She thought about that for a minute before responding.

Finally she said, "With your help, I have had a lot of shifts in perspectives in a number of areas of the business. There are a lot of myths and misconceptions out there that we company owners believe to be true. All they do is limit us in getting what we want from our business. It is tricky enough to grow a business without these misguided notions getting in our way.

"My perspectives have changed in so many ways. I have always been willing to work hard, and to do what it takes to reach my goals. But I think very differently about business and growing now, than I did three years ago.

"After achieving what my team and I have accomplished over these past three to four years, I know that it is realistically possible to grow a business substantially, without killing myself or completely losing my freedom over it. In fact, it has been really fun and very rewarding.

"I'm still amazed that we will be five times bigger by the end of this year than we were only four short years ago."

"That's very exciting, Louise!"

"Exactly! And you know what?" she added. "We're just getting started!"

"I believe it. So why do you think that more business owners don't do it?" I asked.

Louise paused, considered my question, and then responded.

"Because owners don't know how to go about it," she said. "It's kind of like seeing a wonderful vision in the sky above you, but no ladder to connect you from the earth to the sky. People only know what they know and growing a business can feel a bit like stepping into the unknown if there is no structure in place. It can be scary and takes courage. It also takes a shift in mindset and different actions from what most people do … certainly different from what I was doing four years ago. And I know that I will have to shift again, moving forward, to achieve the next level of growth for the company."

"Yes, you will," I responded, acknowledging the continually changing growth path. "The good news is that with those shifts, you *really can* get what you want from your business."

"I agree," she said. "Most business owners that I know don't do it. We don't see the natural traps that are there, so we fall right into them, and then we get stuck.

"I have had to rethink almost every major part of my business to achieve the level of growth we have seen," she added.

THINKING BIG IS NOT ENOUGH

Many entrepreneurs believe that to grow a company really big, you just need to think in much bigger terms. If only that were true! There is much more to growth than that.

"It does take a different mindset to generate large-scale growth," I asserted. "Thinking big is not enough.

"What I find is that business owners work really hard, and their businesses grow to a certain level. That's when they start to hit a wall, where everything just seems to get harder. They either end up on a plateau, or on a bit of a roller coaster, with sales going up and down."

"I have seen and felt that," Louise commented. "It seems that many owners either fear growth, having tried it and run into huge obstacles, or they just get tired of the constant issues and swings that hit them as they try to scale things."

"You got that right," I said.

"There is also no silver bullet," she added. "At least I haven't found one."

BUSINESS GROWTH: THREE COMMON STRATEGIES

Growing a business can be tricky. There are multiple moving parts. When Louise had first gone looking for information and support, she knew she needed outside help and wanted to find the right resources for herself and her company.

She had found many people in the market purporting to be business growth experts who, in reality, didn't know what it was like to grow a business from the ground up.

These experts were in many ways, the "one plate spinner" consultants referred to in Chapter 1, with experience in only one particular area. Louise and Kate had interviewed advisor experts who were ex-bank managers, ex-marketing managers, and successful big-business people who came from large organizations. She felt they only had a partial view or a skewed view of what it was like within a small and growing business. Therefore, she found that their advice was only of limited value to her in her situation.

"When I was looking for possible resources, before we first connected," said Louise, "I found that much of what was available fell into three categories of advice on business growth."

"And what were these?" I asked.

The Silver Bullet

"The first type is what I call 'The Silver Bullet,'" Louise explained. "Here is the magic formula, the secret to a business owner's issues. Follow this formula and everything will work brilliantly!"

"But I thought you just said you haven't found a silver bullet yet," I commented.

"I haven't," she said. "But that doesn't mean that those theories aren't out there, purporting to do magic. When I mentally applied them to what we were doing at Sponge, I knew they just wouldn't work for my business."

"Well," I observed, "sometimes a formula does work, and it certainly worked for the proponent of that particular system, whatever it may be. However, since each person and each business is unique, it doesn't work all the time. Hence, it's not really a silver bullet."

"Exactly!" Louise said.

"Don't get me wrong," she added. "There's a lot of good information out there. It just gets to be so much, it can be confusing. If it doesn't fit, it can be a waste of time and resources."

"So what are the other types of advice you came across?" I asked.

Armageddon Theory

Louise continued. "The second type is the 'Armageddon Theory.' According to the advice in this category, everything you have done or learned so far in business is now wrong, and needs to be blown up or otherwise discarded, because in this new environment, here is the new reality of life, or the 'Real Truth.' This is usually accompanied by a 'silver bullet' strategy or formula that we just talked about.

"I must admit that after the recession, when the bank cut our line of credit in half, I was wondering if everything had permanently changed."

"Sometimes there are permanent changes that occur," I said.

Louise agreed. "But even as the world changes, there are always ways to move forward and make things work. If I accepted that my previous experience was useless because of some new reality, then I would be left just looking for that silver bullet again, and I don't think it exists. Or I should get out of business altogether, and I'm certainly not ready to do that!"

"So what was the third type you encountered?" I asked.

Half Truths Presented as Truths

"This was the most interesting of them all," she said. "This is what I call 'Half Truths Presented as Truths.'"

"Have you got an example of that one?" I asked.

"Sure," she said. "'Do what you love and the money will follow. Just follow your passion and it will all work out.' The 'follow your passion' formula is very popular, and to an extent it makes sense, unless it is presented as the complete picture.

"I recently got into a conversation with a woman who owned a small business, who had doubts about this theory after trying it. She had been struggling in her business, and after reading all about following her passion, she started focusing on just one aspect of her business—making the product itself. That's what she loved to do.

"Needless to say, even though she found that part of the experience quite rewarding, her business suffered from her lack of focus on sales and on cash flow. To make a long story short, the money didn't follow. Instead, the money went away, and so did her business."

"I get the point," I replied. "Clearly, incomplete theories can either lead people astray, or they lack credibility and don't get implemented, merely because they are incomplete.

"To achieve success in business, it really is more about shifting a large number of little things in a variety of different areas that add up to making a big collective difference."

"Yes," she agreed. "Like what we have built here at Sponge: more sales, more profits, and a happy, productive, engaged team of great people making a difference for our customers."

"The work we have done together so far has worked for you, Louise," I stated. "Into which of the three categories would you place our work?"

"I think that you are in a fourth category," she said. "Let me think about that and get back to you."

27

"I look forward to hearing your thoughts on that," I commented, smiling.

The Three-Year Review: Getting Started

With this visit, Louise really wanted to paint the picture for her next level of growth. In order to accomplish this, I suggested that we review what had been accomplished over the past three years. This would provide her with the foundation she would need to take the next steps.

"Michael, there have been so many changes that we have made, it may be hard to review them all," Louise commented. "Let's do this methodically."

She added, "I would suggest that we look at it from the perspective of one of the business models that we have used as we have grown, breaking down each of the pieces, but we have used a few different versions of business models as we have grown over the past few years, and that might get confusing."

"Why do you have different business models, anyway?" she asked me. "Don't most consultants have just one formula to follow?"

I chuckled. "Louise, if I were to just go with a single formula, wouldn't that just be a different 'silver bullet'?"

Different Sized Businesses Need Different Models

I went on to explain why there is no one formula that works for all businesses and why I use different business models for different sized businesses.

"Different businesses are all different sizes, and different dynamics apply at each stage of development," I stated. "We have one approach for the micro-business, another one for a company that is a bit bigger, and it continues to evolve through the varying sizes of businesses we support, including very different strategies for businesses in the tens of millions in sales.

"Instead of making a company fit some arbitrary model, I have developed things in a modular format, and within each different area, there are differing levels of depth, for companies of differing sizes and circumstances. That way, we can meet our clients where they are, and we continue to be effective as an outside resource as they grow."

"That sounds very complicated," Louise said. "It didn't feel like that to me as we worked through things. You basically just showed me a framework and we worked with it. But it wasn't a step-by-step system. It was different somehow. You definitely brought structure to our conversations, but it felt to me to be more organic."

"When I think of it," I said, "I think back to my youngest child, Kathleen, who was extremely bright and also getting herself in trouble in school, even in Grade 1. It turns out that these two details were linked. Lots of gifted kids don't want to sit still while others are learning, so they end up getting in trouble. When my wife and I discovered what the real issue was, we looked around, and found her a private school for gifted kids in town.

"There were twenty students in the whole school, and they varied from Grade 1 through Grade 7. Every student had gifts in different areas. As a result, at the school, they customized each subject for each child. So a Grade 3 student might have Grade 2 equivalent reading, but a Grade 12 equivalent capacity in math. By customizing every subject to each child, they could take scholastic competition away, and allow the children to otherwise learn to socialize normally. Kathleen excelled in that environment."

"That sounds like an exceptional school!" Louise remarked.

"It was," I agreed. "I figured that if they could do that for a child's education, why couldn't I come up with a matrix of customized processes for businesses developed in layered modules. By building our processes in this way, we can meet owners where they are at, rather than making them contort to a formula that may not fit. Also, we can train our consultants on how to go to their clients where they are at as well.

"The whole idea behind our modular approach has been to make it simple for you, while still being relevant to exactly where your business is, at different times. It's a bit complicated for us, but by breaking things down, we have evolved our own systems to support that level of customization."

"I must admit that it has felt seamless to me over these past three years," commented Louise.

"The strategies we need to use with a company going from 30 million to 100 million," I continued, "are quite different from the tools that would be useful to a business growing from 2 million to 10 million. These are again different from those for a company of less than 1 million in sales."

"So Michael, is that in Dollars or Pounds Sterling?" Louise asked with a wry smile.

"If you keep going the way you intend, within the next few years you will have Kate opening up that New York office, and then you can have it in both currencies," I replied.

"I like that thought," she said. "Okay. Now I can tell you what that *fourth category* of business advice is. At least I can describe my experience of our work."

I waited, expectantly.

The Gardener

Louise went on to explain.

"There is a lot of information out there, and a number of people with a magic formula that we talked about. But there is a problem with a formula. It doesn't really take into account in detail your situation and challenges. It is a bit like a doctor prescribing medicine when he hasn't understood the patient's problem thoroughly. It may be okay, but more likely it will be a formula for disaster.

"As we started working together, I realized you weren't about any formula but about creating the right conditions for growth—the right people, processes, and structures.

"Michael, your approach was more like a 'gardener' tending to a plant. Sometimes it needed more water, soil improver, or sun. And to a Master Gardener, each plant is a little bit different, and needs a little bit different level of care, based upon its unique needs.

"Your focus was on making continuous small improvements. And every little growth we experienced, we celebrated. Soon, these 'little growths' started to add up to 'big growths.' I don't know if that puts you in a different category, but that is what I experienced in our time together.

"I guess that makes it a bit difficult to do a systematic review," she added.

"Not at all," I said and offered Louise a possible approach for our review.

"If I had to summarize our work together, we have focused on a number of core aspects of business growth. However, these may easily fit into three basic categories. Let's review things from these three aspects:

1. **the underlying structures of your business,**
2. **your people, and**
3. **sales and marketing.**"

"Sounds like a plan," she said.

With that, Louise and I began our three-year review.

Section 1: Structures

"*Companies that grow for the sake of growth or that expand into areas outside their core business strategy often stumble. On the other hand, companies that build scale for the benefit of their customers and shareholders more often succeed over time.*"
Jamie Dimon, President and CEO of JPMorgan Chase

3 PLANNING FOR GROWTH

"If I had five minutes to chop down a tree, I'd spend two and a half sharpening my ax."
Unknown[3]

In discussing Louise's achievements over these past three years, we identified a number of areas of progress.

Even on that first train ride, three years ago, we talked through a high-level game plan for large-scale growth.

LOUISE'S REFLECTIONS ON GROWING HER BUSINESS

"I knew I wanted to grow the business. For years, I knew it. I could see clearly by the international clients we were winning that the potential was there. I just didn't know how to go about doing it.

"I didn't have a lot of time to think or plan how I could do it, because I was so involved with my day-to-day work—making sales, overseeing production, keeping a close eye on finances,

---

[3]This quote is often attributed to Abraham Lincoln. However, the true origin is not known.

35

and planning marketing activities. I knew relying on past experience wasn't going to get me there. What I had done had gotten me as far as I was at that time. Doing more of the same things we were doing wasn't going to get me too much farther. This was just going to generate the same results. I felt we were on a plateau.

"Copying competitors wasn't an option. I didn't want to be like them. I wanted to have a distinct voice in the elearning industry.

"So this dream felt like kind of a pipe dream, something that was going to happen in the future. Until I thought, *What if the future is closer than I think? What if the future was tomorrow or even the next hour and not just a big nebulous expanse of time ahead of me?* I was excited for the future, but I was also frustrated, because I couldn't see a way through. Unlike the woman who blindly followed the advice to 'Do what you love and the money will follow,' I knew that wouldn't work for me.

"That's when I started to research how to grow businesses and how entrepreneurs did it. That led to where we are today."

As I was listening to Louise talk about her experience, I was reminded of what she had intuitively known that many business owners overlook. That productivity is a function of design and structure, not our good intentions or our big thoughts and dreams. We can be as well intended or as "Big Picture" as we like. By itself, it still won't make a difference if the appropriate structures are not in place to support us.

No matter how much I intended to go to Europe or dreamt of it, without access to an appropriate structure—a flight or passage on a boat—I would not get there.

MYTHS VERSUS MISCONCEPTIONS

As we began the three-year review, Louise and I recalled the many myths and misconceptions she had encountered along the way. We also discussed the shifts in perspective that she had upon realizing many of the ideas she thought were true about building a business were in fact hindering her ability to do so.

Myths are notions that are either just inaccurate or ideas that may have worked at one time or in some situations, and then somehow were turned into a rule to be followed indiscriminately. We continue to follow these "rules," even when the circumstances change and they no longer apply.

Misconceptions are not necessarily inaccurate. However, they are either incomplete or misapplied.

I recall Louise saying, "With all the juggling we do as owners, we tend to latch onto anything that seems like it might help. Is it any surprise that we have as many misconceptions about what's true and what's not in business?

"As a business owner, I just want my business venture to work. Whatever helps me, I will embrace."

"Yes," I agreed. "But if we hit enough that doesn't pan out, we start to get resigned and cynical.

"Some of us doubt ourselves. Others stop trusting outsiders. We go to what we know, and we dig in and work harder. At least we will know what we are doing, and there's nobody to blame but ourselves if it doesn't work out."

"So why can't 'Do what you Love' work?" she asked.

"It can and does work," I responded. "However, it is only one half of a two-part formula. The first part is Vision and the second is Structure. As we discussed earlier, under-structured companies don't do well. They go through lots of pain, and many fail."

> **Misconception: Do what you love and the money will follow (or, follow your passion).**

Following your passion is definitely one of the ingredients to business success, but it is a misconception because it is only part of the story.

"What do you mean it is only part of the story?" Louise asked. "I thought that this theory was simply untrue."

"No," I responded. "I believe it is true. Your passion is very important to business growth. Many people follow their passion and things work out well. The reason I call it a misconception is that there is more to the story than that. Like in the situation of the friend you described, by itself, passion—or vision—doesn't give you enough.

"That's like asking where electricity comes from and someone pointing to the plug in the wall. This may be true. Electricity does come from the plug in the wall, at least if the plug is active. But there is more to the story than that. Someone else might say that electricity comes from the wired pole in the street. That may also be true, but again, there is more to the story than that.

"The more we understand the game behind the game, the easier it is to determine when some rule or guideline might apply and when it doesn't fit."

> **Perspective Shift: Productivity is a function of design and structure.**

To truly understand business growth, or anything for that matter, you need to understand what goes on in the background. I call that "the game behind the game." Others call it the "root cause."

The Game Behind the Game

The better our understanding of what is in the background or how things really work at their core, the better we can predict the outcomes of changes or shifts. Much of the work in growing a business or achieving any complex goal is to gain access to that "behind-the-scenes" picture, so that we can see what is coming.

The clearer we are about the drivers of the various elements of a business, and how they interplay at different sizes, the more access we have to determining the appropriate steps to achieve our goals for growth.

Most of what Louise and I had to address was what was going on "behind the scenes." We needed to work on the underlying structures that impact business growth and profitability, and ultimately, an owner's freedom.

We discussed more of the dynamics that people face as they seek to grow their companies.

THE NORMAL CYCLE OF GROWTH

As a company grows, it tends to outstrip its structures. As owners, we see that we have extra capacity in a number of areas. What we often fail to notice is when we are at or near our capacity limits. Staffing is where we are often at our limit from a capacity perspective.

We generally don't carry a great deal of extra capacity in our staffing. After all, if someone isn't fully utilized, either we combine jobs to work with fewer people, or we find productive things for them to do. Otherwise, we feel overstaffed, and that is just money leaking out the door. That is just bad business practice and very expensive.

When there is a new task to do that only takes a few hours per week, we won't hire a whole other person to deal with this. Instead, we just ask one of our resourceful staff to handle the new activity.

Surely, this can be fit into the regular routine. In fact, it may only be an hour every other week. This should be nothing at all for one of our highly competent people to handle.

And that is how it happens.

As we grow and outstrip those human resources structures, we invariably experience pain. People get stretched thin. Sometimes they manage things well. Every now and then, someone drops the ball. Sometimes, someone gets fed up and quits. The rest of the staff suck it up and work through the strain, doing the best they can.

If the pain gets too much, we sometimes shrink back to our former size, declaring, *I'll never try that again!*

This leads us to a common misconception in business.

Misconception: The easiest and safest way to grow is by aiming for 10 percent to 15 percent annual growth.

While it may be true that we will eventually achieve that 10 or 15 percent growth, it is usually the more painful way to go.

Perspective Shift: It is often easier to double or triple revenues, than to achieve consistent 10 percent to 15 percent annual growth.

When we plan to double or triple our business, we don't delude ourselves into thinking that the current structures will do the job. We realize that we will need to add new structures, and bolster or overhaul existing ones.

With this clarity in hand, we merely think through the shifts that are needed, and prepare for the eventual changes that we will experience.

Louise had experienced this perspective shift for herself.

"I recall having a meeting with our accountant a few years ago to review our annual accounts. He made the comment that we had a good year, growing by 15 percent. Having now experienced growth of over 80 percent in one year, I realize that 15 percent was really little more than standing still—not enough to fund any real changes, take on more staff, or develop the business."

"Louise, in your case," I commented, "you saw additional potential capacity in module design and development, even three years ago. As long as the instructional design was done well, a small increase should have been easy to handle for your people.

"But what happened as you increased sales, even before we started working together?"

Louise pondered this for a moment.

"Kate, who was handling sales with me, had to step in and help with the instructional design," she replied. "She has always been really good at this, but that would take her out of sales for periods of time. In turn, our sales levels were inconsistent, while running both Kate and me ragged. Instructional Design has been one role we have had a tough time filling with quality internal staff."

"Some version of that is what happens to most businesses," I commented. "Because capacity levels are not uniform across all the different areas of a business, as a company grows it really does outstrip some of its structures. That's the pain that companies experience that I was talking about."

"Well, we sure felt it," remarked Louise. "Poor Kate was spread very thin, and that also increased the pressure on me to take on more of the sales myself, all while managing cash flow with Matt, and managing our deliverables.

"It felt like one of those circus fire drills, with all the clowns running in circles around a fire that nobody is extinguishing."

I explained to Louise that as business owners, when we experience the pain of growing, we either shrink back to our previous levels (often vowing to never grow again), or we limp along in a series of ups and downs. These swings are sometimes painful and only briefly satisfying. Eventually, we catch up our structures to support our increased size.

Then we grow again ... and the cycle continues.

"That sounds pretty much like what we had experienced," said Louise. "That's also why I had thought the direction of that first exercise you had me answer on our first train ride three years ago, about exploring what I had originally thought was exorbitant growth at the time was a bit odd. Rather than stopping to fix things, we explored even bigger growth than I had previously imagined.

"That points to another misconception I had, and a change in perspective I gained. I thought that before looking at growth, I had to fix and move past the difficulties I was encountering at the time. Only once everything was fixed, could I consider growing."

> **Misconception: I have to fix and move past current difficulties before I start looking at growth.**

"Is this never true?" she asked.

"Sometimes there are things to fix first," I responded. "However, in your case it was not a big deal, because you and your people were delivering great results to your customers."

"Yes, so?" she queried.

When Growth Is a Bad Idea

If we can't deliver powerfully to our customers at our current size, it is not a good idea to try to grow until this is fixed. Otherwise, we will only accelerate the rate at which we let the marketplace know how bad we are. That's never good.

> **Perspective Shift: If I currently deliver quality results to clients and customers, I may be able to grow now.**

People have long memories. If they don't get value, they vote with their feet. They just turn away from us and move to a competitor. And it will be a long time before they try us again, if ever. Before we attempt to grow, we need to make sure we are delivering something that satisfies our customers. Without happy customers at our current size, growth can be next to impossible to achieve effectively.

That part of fixing and stabilizing is definitely true. However, planning for growth, then growing and stabilizing along the way, allows us the extra funding—from sales—to be able to afford the increased structures needed to firm up our companies as we grow.

This may sound like a lot of juggling, and it is. Yet, that is what helped Louise fund her company's growth. Annual growth rates of 80 percent certainly made it easier financially to handle things along the way.

THE BIGGER PICTURE

Louise commented, "Even though I didn't expect it, I must admit that the conversation that we had about growth during your first visit, three years ago, made a big difference for me.

"After telling you that I hoped to achieve £600 thousand in the current year (we actually achieved £700 thousand that year), we went on to explore what £6 million might look like, sometime in the future.

"You were right when you said that this exercise was simply like MBA math. It wasn't actually that hard to develop the snapshot of how a company such as ours would be structured at that higher level of turnover."

The number of elearning modules and the number of production staff needed was straightforward, since Louise knew what it took to do one full module of an average sized sale. The rest was just multiplying it out. We guessed at the finance and admin support staffing needs, but Louise was clear on the sales per person, and as a result, the total number of salespeople that would be needed.

"The whole thing was easier than I thought it would be," Louise said.

"It's not that hard, when you take the time to figure it out. We did have a three-and-a-half hour train ride to sort things through," I commented, with a smile.

She replied, "Yes, and by going through that, I really did start to think that a large level of growth was possible, though I still had trouble getting my head around it.

"Then, when we cut that in half to £3 million, thinking through all the elements needed to have a fully functional company at that smaller size, that was a number I could see.

"This led me to the first of a number of shifts in perspective on that trip. I always thought that when planning for growth, you start with today, doing a SWOT analysis [SWOT is a tool to analyze a company's Strengths, Weaknesses, Opportunities, and Threats], and then grow things out from the present forward."

"That's a pretty common assumption, even though, in my

opinion, it is often ineffective for small businesses," I said. "Don't get me wrong. I don't have an issue with the SWOT analysis itself. However, it is most effective in a big business environment, where a number of parties doing planning together need to get clear on what they have. Most small business owners are very clear on their situation, as they live it each day."

I could tell that this intrigued Louise, so I continued, "I rarely spend time with the SWOT. It is a 'nice-to-have', not a 'need-to-have'. Too many people have treated that tool like it was essential, or like magic or something, but they don't go deep enough to make it useful. If we are unclear, then sure, let's get clear. But otherwise, there are better tools for a business owner to use to grow."

Myth: Planning for growth is the same, no matter what size business you have.

"One of the common mistakes that most people make is to treat a small or medium-sized business the same as a big business, only scaled down. It's just not correct or useful," I said and explained further.

"It's like comparing a cruise ship to a little speed boat. Yes, they are both boats, and they both float. However, if you put them out into the ocean and you stir up a bit of weather, let's see how the captains would operate."

"How do you think they would differ?" I asked.

Louise thought about this for a moment.

"Well," she said, "the captain of a cruise ship might never touch the controls of the ship. She would have a whole crew to steer and steady the ship."

"Yes, she would," I said. "At least, that's how I'd imagine it."

"How about the guy running the speed boat?" I asked.

"Out in rough weather in the middle of the ocean? I wouldn't want to be him! Unless he has one hand on the steering wheel, and the other on the bailer, he's in for a load of trouble!" she replied.

"Louise, you have just quite eloquently described the life, and the predicament, of owners of most small to medium-sized businesses."

> **Perspective Shift: The biggest threat to the owners of small to medium- sized businesses is time.**

Unless the company is big enough to afford many additional resources, a business owner's biggest threat is time. There always seems to be too much to do and not enough time to do it. And because small to medium-sized businesses are not stuffed with cash, the financial reserves to have a sufficient crew to handle everything that needs to be handled are not usually available.

Even in situations where owners have large financial reserves, spending money needs to be balanced against sales and profits. Otherwise, a financial reserve just shrinks, and eventually goes away.

The shift in perspective is to treat a small to medium-sized business differently from the traditional big business. That includes the planning.

> **Myth: Planning is best done from the present to the future.**

"The other myth that you pointed to, Louise, was that planning for growth is best done by looking from the present into the future. As you recall, that was not the way we planned things for you and your business, was it?" I asked.

"It certainly wasn't, though that was a hard habit to break," she replied.

"In my experience," I said, "the approach of moving from the present to the future is full of traps."

"That sounds ominous," she commented. "What do you mean?"

"First of all," I explained, "when I look forward, I know that the future is uncertain, so my mind gets caught up in worrying about whether I can overcome a number of stumbling blocks to achieving my goals.

"Secondly, the difficulty with looking from the present to a larger future is that it forces me to look from a smaller picture to a bigger one. I am more likely to miss things looking from smaller to larger."

Perspective Shift: Planning is best done from the larger future to the present.

"If, on the other hand," I continued, "I start with the future, larger picture, thinking that I have already achieved it, my brain operates from that perspective. It is easy to imagine things with certainty. I just act as if I am in the future, and then look back and see how I did it. My brain assumes that I have already overcome the stumbling blocks."

"It sounds crazy when you explain it," she said. "But I experienced it in real life, and I did find that it worked quite well," she said. "I guess that is why 'Visioning' works."

"Exactly!" I said, "Tricking our brains into thinking we have already overcome whatever obstacles might surface makes all the difference in the world. Looking from the bigger picture to the smaller one, say from £6 million to £3 million, was far easier for you, wasn't it?"

"It wasn't hard at all, because we had already thought

everything out for the £6 million version of the business," she concurred.

"We are taking things out that were already identified, instead of guessing what we might be missing," I explained. "The key is as long as we are thorough enough at the largest picture, taking things, resources, possibly locations, and people out of the equation misses fewer things.

"The more prepared we are for growth, with the appropriate structures identified, the less likely it will be that we outstrip our structures and endure the pain that comes with that."

"It certainly has been eventful," Louise said, "but I wouldn't say it was painful, except for a few spots, but I'm sure we will get to that as we continue our review.

"What I noticed was that once we got down to £3 million in sales, we switched gears and went back to the £400 thousand we had done the previous year, and started building out from there."

"You had already identified enough of the structures that you needed to build into your growth plan," I said, "so it was time to identify some specific, concrete steps that you could take to get started.

"It's one thing to see the bigger picture, but that, by itself can be daunting. Remember, thinking big is not enough. By breaking things down to a few steps to start, you start to gain some wins and start to gain a feeling of momentum as you generate that initial progress."

"Yes," she agreed. "Moving to small initial steps made a big difference for us in those early days."

As we continued our review, we moved to analyzing the shifts in Louise's role as the company has grown.

Summary of Myths and Misconceptions

1. Misconception: Do what you love and the money will follow.
2. Misconception: The easiest and safest way to grow is by aiming for 10 percent to 15 percent annual growth.
3. Misconception: I have to fix and move past current difficulties before I start looking at growth.
4. Myth: Planning for growth is the same, no matter what size business you have.
5. Myth: Planning is best done from the present to the future.

Summary of Perspective Shifts

1. Productivity is a function of design and structure.
2. It is often easier to double or triple revenues than to achieve consistent 10 percent to 15 percent annual growth.
3. If I currently deliver quality results to clients and customers, I may be able to grow now.
4. The biggest threat to the owners of small to medium-sized businesses is time.
5. Planning is best done from the larger future to the present.

4 THE EVOLVING ROLE OF THE OWNER

"For fast-acting relief, try slowing down."
Written by Jane Wagner for Lily Tomlin, Actress and Comedian

FREEING LOUISE UP TO GROW THE BUSINESS

Clarity allows access to action. The clearer you are, the less that needs to be said.

There are ways to approach business strategy that make it harder on people, and there are ways to make it easier, and more effective, at the same time.

What's the game-behind-the-game, you ask? Good question!

The *game* behind the game in this case is our old friend— human behaviour. The more we understand about how we think and how our brains work, even a little bit, the better we are able to choose a planning approach that will serve us.

This is one of the areas of change that surprised Louise. She wasn't quite sure what to expect, but she didn't expect to go where we went.

"Michael, when you first visited," said Louise, "you asked me to describe all my roles, as well as what I really enjoyed doing. I found this really hard to answer. I didn't really distinguish between roles. I just got on with what needed to be done. In fact, I was doing a bit of everything—sales, marketing, instructional design, project management, and finance.

"I was very competent at doing different roles, prioritizing my time, and making sure that I did them thoroughly and to the best of my abilities."

The problem with being a capable person (yes, being a capable person can actually be a problem) is that we can still only do as much as we can, within the time we have. However, because we are so capable, we tend to rely on our own skills to get the job done, rather than looking for methods beyond ourselves.

If Louise had a client call, a project plan, and a tender to get out in a day, she was good at managing her time, but the quality of output was limited by the amount of time she could spend on each priority.

"It never really occurred to me that for things to change, I would have to change," she said.

"There was one thing you said, right at the start, though, that caught my attention. When we were looking at a bigger future, you asked me what I would be doing ... what my role would be, as part of that bigger picture. That was a really tough question for me.

"That was also the first time it occurred to me that my role would need to change, and fairly significantly. Once you asked the question, it became obvious, but until that time, I never really thought much about it. I kind of figured that my job would be the same, but that I would just be doing more of it."

> **Myth: As I grow, my job will stay the same. I'll just be doing more of it.**

In fact, just the opposite is true. I knew that nothing in the company would really change, until Louise started to change her focus. She would need to determine what her new role would be within the company—her new job.

This leads to another myth that most business owners have. Actually, it is more of a fear they harbor.

> **Myth: To grow my business, I will have to work harder.**

As entrepreneurs, it is very common for us to take an either/or approach. Either we look for that silver bullet, or we believe that we have to work harder to grow. This either/or thinking causes people a great deal of unnecessary pain. When I first met Louise, she was struggling with this dilemma and experiencing that pain.

"Over the last three years," recalled Louise, "my role has been a question I have often come back to. I know that I need to think of my role as continuously evolving as the business grows to ensure that I am doing activities that make a real difference.

"I must admit though that when we first started, I found your approach very different from what I expected.

"When we first met, the bank had just cut our line of credit in half. I was juggling our cash flow with our sales and production requirements. It was very tiring, constantly looking to convert new clients from the website inquiries we were getting, as well as seeking repeat business from our existing clients. Both Kate and I were spread pretty thin."

"Paper thin, if I recall," I added.

"Yes," she agreed. "At the same time as this, I was pushing our people to stay on top of clients who frequently ran into delays in getting us what we needed to complete their modules. We needed client sign-off to be able to invoice and get paid. With cash flow tight, this was a constant battle … quite a juggling act. I was hoping for answers to these problems.

"But you didn't go there at all. We were only five minutes into that first train ride and you headed in a completely different direction."

Yes," I agreed. "You were running yourself ragged, and feeling frustration. You didn't need some outsider who didn't know your business as well as you did to tell you what to do about your day-to-day issues. You really needed to think about your business differently."

> **Perspective Shift: Beyond a certain point, doing more of the same activities can impede growth.**

We can't just do more of the same thing and expect our businesses to grow. Change is required. Yet, as business owners, we try this strategy far too frequently. After all, to get to our initial levels of success, we encountered adversity and muscled through to gain the desired results. This is how most companies grow at the start. Yet, that strategy will only work for so long.

"Eventually business owners will hit a wall. There is only so much an owner can handle on their own," I said.

"Is there one wall for all business owners or is it different for different companies?" Louise asked. "What have you found in working with different types and sizes of companies?"

"It varies by industry, by company, and by individual entrepreneur," I replied. "We each have different capacity levels.

"We had one micro-business owner in Canada who came to us, having hit the edge of her capacity at $80 thousand in gross revenues per year. We've seen companies in Canada and the US hit that wall at the $300 thousand to $500 thousand in annual revenues."

"Is it just smaller companies that get stuck, or do you see this with bigger ones as well?" she asked.

"Companies can hit that wall at any level of revenue; it depends on the industry and the type of business. People hit plateaus at different levels of growth too," I replied, "and for different reasons.

"One client in the construction industry approached us after plateauing at $10 million for two years, with almost no net income. Another company, also in construction, was actively and intentionally shrinking after hitting $14 million in sales the previous year. Both companies were under-structured. As a result, they were unable to grow beyond their previous sales levels. Both companies required major restructuring. Once they had enough of the right people and processes in place, they were both able to generate sustainable profits and move to the next level.

"We had one business owner of a propane company who came to us while operating at the edge of his capacity, with his sales at $12 million per year. He had very little net income ($60 thousand net), and his accountant was still operating with a manual, paper-based bookkeeping system. The fact that this owner could operate at that level of sales with a product with such tiny margins (8 to 9 cents per litre or sometimes even less) was amazing. He was literally working a $12 million company with tiny margins out of his head."

"That's pretty impressive," Louise remarked. "Though what's the point of running a company that big and not making a profit," she added.

"It didn't take much to help him achieve increased profits," I said. "By helping him to automate his finance department and then identifying the sources of leakage, he was able to increase his profits to nearly $750,000 per year within two years."

"What stopped him from doing this earlier?" she asked.

"There were two things," I responded. "First of all, he was a man in his late fifties with a high level of regard and trust in his dear old friend, who had run the finance department for almost thirty years. There was a level of trust and respect there, and the owner didn't want to displace him when he was so close to retiring, despite knowing that things were not as tight as they could be. To change the system meant he had to push his dear friend into retirement.

"As business owners, we often feel a sense of loyalty to those who have been with us from the beginning. In this case, the owner didn't realize just how much this was costing him.

"Secondly, he was caught in all the same types of traps that catch most business owners. His business had grown more complex and while he could keep track of most things, he had outgrown his structures. This included the structural trap of not changing his role to a more strategic one, as his company grew."

"What happened to the friend?" asked Louise.

"The owner had a chat with him," I replied, "and the friend, in his late sixties, retired, allowing the second in command of that department to take over and automate the finance department."

> **Perspective Shift: The bigger the game gets, the more we are paid to THINK, and the less we are paid to DO.**

In a growing business, there are many moving pieces at work, and they are getting more and more complex as the company grows. The only way to get on top of the growth of the company is to see all the moving pieces collectively as a system, and to view that system as it works in a continually shifting marketplace (See Figure 4.1).

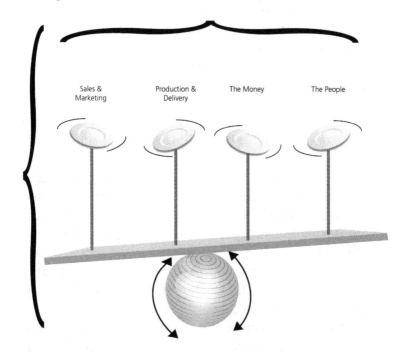

Figure 4.1 - An owner needs to focus from above, and from the side, to get the full view of the business as one system within a fluid marketplace.

It is only by looking at the whole thing as one system that, as business owners, we may successfully navigate our way to increasingly higher levels of growth, profit, and freedom.

Louise remarked, "When you had me identify all my roles and duties, I noticed just how much I was doing that I could pass along to others. I also saw which things I needed to keep and continue to address. By going through this exercise, I was able to start freeing up my time to focus on the higher leverage activities within the business.

"Hiring that first production support person was really important to me. Dan was able to take lots off my plate and address the items in a very focused and complete manner. He has since moved into the Project Management team, gained qualifications in project management, and he has really grown to be one of our core project managers. He leads the group with translation services of our elearning modules into different languages for clients with staff and customers in countries around the world.

"With Dan's initial level of help, I noticed that far more was possible. I found bandwidth I didn't realize at the time was available.

"By freeing myself up to focus more on the bigger picture, I was able to work more closely with the different departments in support of their respective needs as we grew. This was critical to us in getting to where we are now, but there was so much more than just Dan's help."

"What other things did you pass to others to free yourself up?" I asked her. "And with that, how has life changed for you?"

Louise thought for a moment.

"As I free myself up more and more, I am finding that I am just as busy as I was before, but doing things at a much higher level. As a result, I have a very large impact on the corporate culture of the company, even as we grow.

"In order for me to free myself up though, the managers within the company have had to really step up."

Louise went on to explain.

"Product development is all Kate's now. Before we would work on it together, but today, she not only leads this ongoing initiative, she also does or orchestrates all the legwork and suggests innovations and improvements in a way that makes it easy for me to agree with what she is proposing. She is making great strides, and the quality of our offerings continues to improve with each client engagement we take on. I am really proud of the progress she has been making.

"Kate has also led some other major projects, like the Learning Management System (LMS), and process documentation, in particular with sales and in support of our Instructional Designers. She did all this while doing an MBA, which she just finished, with distinction.

"In the past, I would be the one taking on these initiatives, usually together with Kate. She is leading them now, which frees me up.

"Matt has done such a good job with the finances," she added, "that I don't need to sit on top of cash flow like I used to. In addition to all the regular accounting activities, he has been actively focused on helping us build our financial reserves, while staying ahead of the company's payables. He still sends me over the cash position on a weekly basis, but some weeks I am too busy to meet with him, and neither he nor I stress about it anymore. That has provided a huge boost to my energy levels.

"With Helen, our office manager, who has her own assistant now, all the logistics of the office are being handled effectively. I don't need to focus on that at all.

"It is also great to have increased support in the Marketing department and in Sales. Our Marketing Manager, Emma, is taking ownership of the Marketing department, and Kelly B. has really stepped up in Sales. But we will talk about those departments and people when we get to that part of the review."

"What's your focus now?" I asked. "Are all of your current activities now strategic?"

"I'm not sure about all of them, but certainly most of my work is either developing or following up strategies, or supporting the managers in their roles," she said.

"In addition to strategic work, I focus on our larger clients, on supporting our sales team and on helping with the recruiting of more key staff."

"This is very different from three years ago, when you pretty much did some of everything each day," I commented.

"Yes, looking back I can see that I was good at managing lots of different activities, but probably wasn't spending my time where I should have been," she conceded. "Even though we are bigger now, with more challenges, in a lot of ways it is also easier. It is definitely more enjoyable to come to work each day. I find all this very exciting!"

"Of course, this would not have worked so well had you not increased your time off and energy management," I commented.

TAKING MORE TIME OFF

One of the areas where owners have difficulty is in taking time off to rest and rejuvenate. Somehow we feel that until we have accomplished what we intended to do, we haven't earned the right to take time off. After all, there is still so much to be done, and the buck (or the pound) stops with us.

Myth: Time off is a reward, to be enjoyed after achieving our goals for growth and profit.

This myth couldn't be further from the truth.

For example, a few of our clients also run marathon (42 km) races. One client who was a runner told me about her system. She prepares for a marathon by varying her routine each day of the week, sometimes having small runs (10 km for her is a small run) and once a week she runs a longer one (starting at 15 km in early training, and lengthening these to a maximum of 32 km a couple of weeks before the race). Every week she has at least one day of rest with no running or exercise at all. The closer to the race, the more days off she takes.

I asked her what would happen if she just ran seven days a week. Her comments were clear. "I would fail at the marathon," she said, quite simply. "I would be too tired to do the job well."

> **Perspective Shift: Time off and self-care are critical ingredients of an effective growth strategy.**

Taking Time Off

If you can't take at least a full week off and leave work behind, don't try large-scale growth. It's harder and you won't be thinking clearly enough to make the critical decisions necessary to implement an effective growth strategy.

Thinking clearly takes a clear mind. A clear mind comes from rest. It doesn't come from getting more done. It comes from rest.

"Initially, I didn't even think this was possible," said Louise. "However, once I started getting some of the items off my plate that others could do, I found that the business could run for a while without me.

"The number of holidays I take has now increased threefold so instead of taking ten working days I am taking around thirty-two business days (in addition to weekends and bank holidays). I am also taking my breaks more frequently throughout the year.

"Previously, as a family we would go to Greece where we have a house for ten days in the summer. In some years, I wouldn't go at all because if things weren't going too well, I did not feel I deserved it. I also used to feel really worried about going away, but now I make a real effort to leave work behind and leave my capable team to get on with it.

"Now, we spend five days in Greece in May, another ten days in Greece in July or August, a three-day trip to the Isles of Sicily in October, and ten days in Arizona visiting my sister in March. I also take a few long weekends on Fridays, which adds another four days.

"Occasionally, when on holiday I do need to do a little work

61

(that only I can do), but this is usually planned in before I go, so there are no surprises.

"I look at things far more strategically than I did before. Between freeing myself up and taking more time off, I am much better equipped to steer our way through the growth of the company, as well as still serving and supporting our key clients."

"Was it as easy as you are making it sound?" I inquired.

"No, not at all!" Louise replied. "A few years ago when I would go away, things would start to fall between the cracks. Luckily, Kate covered for me initially. I began to discover structures that were missing. Once I identified them, I could start to fill in with processes. By the time I took my third or fourth holiday, things were much better.

"But, let's be clear," she added. "Those first couple of holidays were pretty stressful."

"If you had it to do again, would you change it?" I asked.

"No way!" she said emphatically. "It was completely worth the initial discomfort. Had I not waded through that learning curve, I never would have reached this point. I am clearer now, and I can tackle complex problems that before I never would have even tried.

"I really now understand the value of rest. It isn't an optional extra, especially when we are working with more complex client situations, continuously recruiting for new staff and growing. Keeping rested enables me to manage the business and cope with all sorts of pressures."

Other Activities for Self-Care

I asked Louise if there were any other activities that she has incorporated into her routine to keep fresh.

"I really love going swimming," she said. "I swim three times a week, usually for about fifty minutes each time. I was doing this long before we met, but only once or twice a week. Now, it is three times a week, like clockwork.

"People sometimes ask me if I find that boring, just going up and down doing laps in the pool. Actually, not at all.

"For me, it is useful, unstructured thinking time. Ideas pop into my head about what I am doing that day, or I may be thinking about a creative approach for a client's elearning programme. Ideas float in and out of my head and when I finish swimming, I feel relaxed and happy.

"This unstructured thinking time is in complete contrast to what I do during the day. I have a daily list of what I want to achieve, which I tick as I go through each item. I have a diary filled with meeting appointments and an inbox with emails that need prioritizing and response.

"So the freedom swimming brings is a real pleasure. Originally, I did it to keep physically fit, but I now realize that the main benefit is in keeping me mentally rested and fit.

"The other thing I do, in the evenings, when I am not travelling, is to take the dog for a walk. Again, this gives me space to have unstructured thinking time and enjoy my surroundings. Just like with swimming, ideas will often just pop into my head and I always feel better for getting out.

"I also enjoy the peace and quiet, which is a big contrast to my day where I am continuously interacting with others. I know that when I am away a lot or very busy and miss my swims or dog walks, my work life is out of balance and I am in danger of not working as effectively as I could be."

"It sounds like those activities are working well for you," I said.

"So far, so good," she said confidently. "Our sales are strong, profits are up, cash flow is healthy, and people are learning."

"Speaking of cash flow and profits, let's go there next," I suggested.

"Sure!" she said. "I have had a few perspective shifts there too."

Summary of Myths and Misconceptions

1. Myth: As I grow, my job will stay the same. I'll just be doing more of it.
2. Myth: To grow my business, I will have to work harder.
3. Myth: Time off is a reward, to be enjoyed only after achieving our goals for growth and profit.

Summary of Perspective Shifts

1. Beyond a certain point, doing more of the same activities can impede growth.
2. The bigger the game gets, the more we are paid to THINK, and the less we are paid to DO.
3. Time off and self-care are critical ingredients of an effective growth strategy.

5 Financial Structures

Louise and I started with a review of the progress made over the past three years in terms of the company's financial situation and the underlying structures that support that part of the company. We reviewed two main areas:
- profitability
- cash flow and financing

Use Financial Structures to Create a Profitable Business

In reviewing the financials three years ago, everything seemed normal for a company of less than half a million pounds per year. Gross profits were decent as a percentage. There was a low net income, but that was really just a function of the small size of the company. It had not yet grown enough to generate a solid net income, over and above pay for Louise and her small team.

Louise had a reasonable facility with her core financial statements. While this is a weak spot for many entrepreneurs,

Louise had a clear understanding of her numbers. With the active support of Matt, her part-time Chief Financial Officer (CFO), this tag-team was very strong right from the start, and that made the job of achieving further progress much easier.

The company's product mix has evolved over the past three years, which is natural for a small and growing business. This supports the goal of growing profits, not just sales.

In our work together, we focused on sales by customer, and eventually Gross Profits (GP) by customer, as we implemented a way of tracking this. At the start, the GP per customer was all over the map, based upon varying input for the various client deliverables. This was smoothed out over time.

Sponge's pricing strategy and inconsistencies in pricing to start (common for companies of this size) were addressed and normalized as the company grew. The pricing strategy was firmed up and is both responsible to clients and consistent for the company now.

"Louise, you have enjoyed a number of solid improvements both with your finances and within your finance department over the past three years," I commented. "Is there anything in particular that stands out for you?"

"Other than going from a position of constantly worrying about cash flow to having money in the bank?" she quipped.

"Yes, other than that," I said with a smile.

"Well, I found that we have so much great information right within our own company history, with the work we have done with clients. By analyzing at a deeper level, I discovered areas where we were losing profits unnecessarily. I also found others where we could have spent more and developed our products and services more quickly or more effectively.

"There is a great deal of information within our finance department. I had always looked at finances as tracking for taxes, my own profit, and monitoring cash flow, so that our staff and suppliers would always be paid on time.

"Even our whole marketing strategy has come from the analysis of our current and past customers. The information had always been there. We just didn't realize what a rich resource it was."

> **Misconception: A company's financial information is mostly used for tax and compliance purposes.**

Too often, entrepreneurs ignore the rich and valuable information within the finance department. One example of this is in determining the profitability of different clients. This information can be most useful in assessing clients with whom it may be otherwise difficult to work. Is it worth it to work with them, or just as difficult financially as it is interpersonally?

When Louise and I first dug into this area, we knew that some clients were a dream to work with, while others were more of a nightmare. These were born out by the numbers as well.

There was a big difference between some frugal clients who watched their investment (happily accepted) and those who wasted the company's time and resources because they didn't know what they wanted, and didn't want to pay for the help to figure it out.

Sure enough, with the help of the company's financial information, we found that many of the interpersonally difficult clients were also not profitable. This made it much easier to decline working with them.

> **Perspective Shift: The finance department can provide rich information to help with growth and increase profit, but only when properly staffed and if the right information is sought.**

A finance department can actually be set up as a profit center. Most people don't understand how this can happen, since there are no revenues generated directly from this department. Yet, if the company is properly staffed to provide the various department managers with the right information, both increases in revenues and decreases in costs can be achieved.

When I first met Louise, Sponge's finance department was primarily responsible for tax and compliance work. Since then Louise and Matt have been actively working on expanding the finance department and further developing Matt's role as Chief Financial Officer. By doing this, the finance department is now able to provide support to each of the revenue-generating departments to increase efficiency and identify further areas of potential revenue growth.

One tool that Louise has used for several years (and still does) is the company's Sales Planner. This tool, which she designed in Excel, combines potential and existing contracts with the anticipated cash receipts for each project within the firm. This has allowed her to stay on top of the company's cash flow—her biggest single point of pain when we first met.

By improving and expanding the finance department, Louise was in a much better position to assess new expenditures as they arose, such as key staff additions and expansion. In 2012 and again in 2014, Sponge had to move to a larger facility to accommodate the growing business.

FINANCING BUSINESS GROWTH

> **Myth: To grow a business, you need major investment capital and investors.**

One of the biggest myths Louise had held to be true—that a business needs investment capital to grow—was easily dispelled in one conversation.

"In the UK," said Louise, "there is a common assumption that any company that wants to grow most likely needs to have one or more investors. The reason for this, business advisors say, is that it is better to have a small slice of a bigger pie than to just have a whole small pie that never grows.

"We were told that very thing from one of the people we interviewed to consult for us, before we chose to work with you. While Kate and I didn't feel there was a good fit between our firm and that consultant, I still thought that this was what we needed to do to grow. TV programmes such as *Dragon's Den*, where you present your business idea to potential investors, help to perpetuate this thinking.

"Michael, when you first came over and we started working together, I assumed that one of your priorities would be to make us investment-ready. I thought we needed somewhere between £100 thousand and £150 thousand from an investor."

"Yes, I remember," I said.

"But it was what else you told me as part of that conversation that I really appreciated," she added and went on to explain.

"You said we could probably grow our business significantly and profitably without an investor. This was a refreshingly different perspective.

"You also said that getting a big lump sum investment can be a bit like a kid in a sweet shop. You can spend the money easily, but if the structures and processes aren't in place to sustain growth, it can be money down the drain. That was a big revelation to me. I always thought having more money was the answer.

"The biggest point you made, which I liked, was that if we could find a way to fund our growth through sales, we wouldn't have to pay it back, nor lose a major equity stake to achieve our goals. That helps me retain the future asset value that is being built."

Perspective Shift: If you grow through sales rather than capital investment, you don't have to pay it back.

"You did, though, recognize that a little bit of extra cash could help us," said Louise. "At the time, our part-time accountant, Matt, was looking to get more involved in our business. You suggested that I negotiate a deal with him so he contributes £15,000 plus agrees to allow access to borrow a bit more if we needed it, for a 10 percent share. This gave us the wiggle room we needed in the short term. It also secured Matt's role as Financial Director and a valued partner. That has been a critical and valuable piece to our growth plans."

It was enough equity to keep Matt interested. It was also a small enough amount of money that it wouldn't hurt him. That and the additional lending that he could (and subsequently did) provide would help the company in the short term, until Louise had the chance to build financial reserves.

"Well, it worked out brilliantly," she asserted. "It was the right deal for all concerned, and helped us out of our cash flow crunch."

One of the biggest mistakes people make when looking at investors is to fail to look at long-term consequences of getting an investor on the wrong terms. It really has to work for both sides, in the short term and in the long term.

One of the worst things Louise could have done was to give

too high a percentage for that small amount of money, and then end up possibly resenting Matt later. That wouldn't have worked for her or for Matt in the long term.

As it is, the working relationship between Louise and Matt has continued to grow stronger over the past few years. He brings a different perspective to Louise and her business, pointing out things that she needs to know, while maintaining that healthy respect for what she brings to the company as its Founder and Managing Director.

This leads to another myth when it comes to investors or partners.

Myth: When bringing on a partner or investor, there is basically one deal to reach. What percentage do they get and for how much money?

One problem that people often have when bringing in an investor is when the investor feels that the financial investment for a minority share gives that person the right to dictate how the company will be run. This can cause endless grief for all concerned.

When bringing in an investor, all the operating parameters need to be set out and well established, in advance, for a financial investment to work well. That occurs more with "passive investors" rather than active partners.

Between and among active partners, there are often disputes, which cause no end of misery in businesses. Fortunately for Louise, she has not had to deal with this issue, but I see it so often in other companies that it is worth bringing up here.

The source of the problem is that there are two separate distinctions that are collapsed when someone thinks of a partner. A partner is both an owner/investor and an officer of the company.

Owners (and equity investors who become owners as well) are the people who take a financial risk for a financial return, both an ongoing return in dividends (if declared), as well as a share in the growth of the asset base of the company. The owners take the financial risks. They are usually the last to get paid. They also get the biggest return for results, when things work well.

Officers of the company, on the other hand, are the people who run the show. They make the decisions and take accountability for the sales, production, finances, and human resources: in short, all aspects of making the company grow. They are paid in accordance with what they deliver as part of their role, based upon their effectiveness as well as the strategic value of that role to the company.

When these two distinctions are collapsed, that is when the trouble begins. If I am an owner/investor, and also working within the company in a role, it works best if I am paid for the role based upon the role's requirements and what a non-owner would get paid (even if deferred due to cash flow constraints). Yet when there are partnership disputes, there is usually confusion in both accountabilities between working partners and a general lack of individual accountability for results from the roles of the respective owners.

In the case of Louise and Matt, Louise handled this intuitively. Matt already had a role within the company before becoming a shareholder. The role didn't change, nor did his pay for that role. The share purchase was kept as a separate issue, and things worked out well for all concerned.

Workload Equality: The Most Common Source of Partner Disputes

Division of labour is the single biggest complaint between partners. When partnerships are not working, this issue is almost always part of the mix.

I hear many different opinions about partnerships, and the reviews are very mixed. The biggest complaint I hear is a lack of equality in the workload between partners.

What follows is a common exchange I hear from business partners who are dissatisfied with their partner's contribution to the business.

Operations Partner: "My partner doesn't pull his share of the work. I am a 50 percent partner, but I do more of the work. He thinks that going out and playing golf with clients constitutes working, while I am in the office slaving my butt off ... It is just not fair."

Selling Partner: "My partner just doesn't get it. These sales don't just walk in the door by themselves. He thinks that because I take the odd client out that somehow I am lounging around, goofing off at the expense of our company, while he slaves away at the office. He doesn't know how many evenings I have to be out, at networking events and client dinners, instead of home with my family. It must be nice to work from 8:00 a.m. to 5:00 p.m. every day, and be able to go home. I know he does a good job, but he does a job. I bring home the bacon. This partnership is not fair."

When Partnerships Work

I spoke with a friend and colleague of mine in Boston, Ken, a fellow consultant who graduated from Harvard University with a Doctorate of Business Administration. He recounted to me the results of a study done there by one of the school's business professors.

Ken told me that a certain professor had co-opted one of his classes to support him in conducting a research study on the drivers of success in business. Apparently, after an exhaustive process of major private and public companies, the only single correlative indicator that aligned consistently with the size and level of business success over time was the number of founding partners. The research found that the higher the number of founding partners, the stronger the companies performed.

In addition to finding this fascinating, I also experienced it directly with many of the various clients with whom I have had the privilege to work over the past twenty years. The more partners, the better they have done.

It is just easier with more committed hands at the table.

The sole practitioners had a rougher go of things, especially in handling the juggling act called business growth.

That doesn't mean that sole owners don't succeed. Many of them just have a tougher time of it.

In the case of Sponge UK, while Louise is the majority shareholder, both Matt and Louise's daughter Kate have a minority interest. Together, they act as very effective supports for each other.

> **Perspective Shift: To avoid difficulties associated with partnerships, separate the roles of owner/investors and officers of the company. Also, sort out all the related issues, not just percentage interests.**

When we operate our partnerships with this in mind, things will go much more smoothly. They will certainly be clearer, and clarity allows access to more effective action.

> **Myth: Other than investors, banks are the only viable sources of funding for a growing business.**

"I was really concerned when the bank cut our operating line of credit in half," recalled Louise. "It had nothing to do with us. Because of the worldwide financial collapse and our economy's recession, the banks were making sweeping changes and either cutting everyone down or cutting them off completely.

"That just made a difficult situation even worse."

"How did you make it work?" I asked.

"As you know," she said, "Matt's money went straight into the company to help out initially. Then we got industrious. Between Matt and me, we found some different programmes and sources of funding, which have all turned out to be of great assistance."

> **Perspective Shift: There are many ways to fund small business growth.**

Louise outlined the many different programmes and sources of funding that she and Matt found to support Sponge's initiatives and the company's growth.

"One of the things we were already doing that helped us with cash flow," said Louise, "was to take deposits and progress payments at different points within each project. By doing this, it meant that we didn't have to wait until the end of an assignment, or thirty to sixty days beyond, to get paid. Without these terms in place, we would have never been able to grow.

"Profit is important, but Cash is King to a business," she added. "I had heard this a lot, but until I started to grow this business significantly, it didn't really register. To us, having our terms of payment set up this way was the difference between being in business and not."

"What are some of Sponge's initiatives you had funded?" I asked.

"Well, we have had quite a few," she said. "I was amazed to find out what non-banking resources exist in our marketplace to support the growth of business, and the development of new products and technologies.

"To fund the development of our Learning Management System (LMS) initiative, we applied for and secured a loan with generous repayment terms through an organization here in England called Funding Circle. This is basically a version of crowdfunding, where a number of people have put together a fund to loan to UK-based companies to support development initiatives. Working with them has been a very easy and quick process—quite refreshing compared with the banks.

"In addition to this, we have also received a development loan from Creative England, a public sector organization committed to support creative UK-based companies, for our Adapt software development project.

"We also applied for and qualified for grants and subsidies for hiring new staff. These came from two sources. One source was the Plymouth University and Western Morning News Growth Fund. This programme covered a portion of some of our new staff's wages for a period of time. This past year we have hired twelve people to get us to our current base of twenty-nine staff. Based on that, we requested and secured subsidies for five of those people.

"The other form of hiring support came from the University of Plymouth-Santander graduate grants, toward employing graduates. These two sources of funding for hiring new staff have certainly made the transition to a larger size much easier."

"You also gained access to training funds for your people, didn't you?" I asked.

"Your leadership training with our staff," said Louise, "was subsidized with a grant from The Growth Accelerator, which was another government-sponsored initiative to support fast-growth companies in this country's down economy."

"You must be the poster-child for success stories with government sources," I said.

Louise just laughed.

"Yes," she said. "I have had my picture in the paper as one of the success stories in this area. But little do they know, the story will continue to get better as we go. We're not done yet. In fact, we are just getting started!"

"That's for sure," I said.

Summary of Myths and Misconceptions

1. Misconception: A company's financial information is mostly used for tax and compliance purposes.
2. Myth: To grow a business, you need major investment capital and investors.
3. Myth: When bringing on a partner/investor, there is basically one deal to reach. What percentage do they get, and for how much money?
4. Myth : Other than investors, banks are the only viable sources of funding for a growing business.

Summary of Perspective Shifts

1. The finance department can provide rich information to help with growth and increase profit, but only when properly staffed and if the right information is sought.
2. If you grow through sales rather than capital investment, you don't have to pay it back.
3. To avoid difficulties associated with partnerships, separate the roles of owner/investors and officers of the company. Also, sort out the related issues, not just percentage interests.
4. There are many ways to fund small business growth.

6 OPERATIONAL STRUCTURES

"To be an enduring, great company, you have to build a mechanism for preventing or solving problems that will long outlast any one individual leader."
Howard Schultz, CEO of Starbucks

Many of Sponge UK's operational structures and processes have been well defined over the past three years. Typical of a small company, they used to work almost exclusively from the personal experience of the various members of the team, rather than from any formally documented systems. Now there are well-defined processes in a number of different departments.

"Operations was one of those areas where I didn't even realize that I had a number of assumptions that just weren't true," commented Louise.

"Were these assumptions more myths or misconceptions?" I asked.

She considered this.

"I think they were more myths," she said.

"For example, I just figured that people knew their jobs, and they would build the tools they needed as they needed them. As a result, there was really no need to actively focus on process development. After all, that's what I do."

PROCESS DEVELOPMENT

> **Myth: People will naturally build the processes they need as they need them.**

"Well, Louise," I ventured to say, "I would suggest that you don't always build these for yourself naturally either. Nobody does. We work with what we have and know, and we don't always realize that there is a better thing available, until it is pointed out.

"You have been working with the Sales Planner you developed for years, haven't you?"

"Yes," she said, still not sure where I was going.

"Do you know the suggestion to add a page to improve the information flow of what you analyze?"

"Yes," she replied. "By adding that extra sheet, I can now tell easily just how much new business each salesperson is securing each month. It made a big difference."

I waited ... and then it came.

"I see," she said, catching my drift. "Are you saying that people—me included—will build processes that we see that are needed, but not the ones we don't see?"

"Exactly!" I replied. "If you don't see it, you won't build it. That's where suggestions from the outside come in handy."

> **Perspective Shift: Process development requires active and consistent focus. Assign someone to be champion for process development.**

As Managing Director of the company, Louise now actively looks for process improvements all the time. With her staff, it is less predictable. Until the people in the company made it a priority, they didn't really have a lot of time to think about how things might be improved internally, or to make the process more streamlined for next time, or documented for future training of additional staff.

However, when Louise made it a priority, and Kate took on being the champion for process improvement, the managers started talking it up and things changed.

In particular, Kate's stepping up supported the other managers to do the same. Then, when each of the managers made it an active priority and were provided additional resources (like scheduling process development time into their day), then it started to improve.

Now, the people at Sponge are identifying potential improvements regularly. Also, managers hold regular meetings where the teams can bring up what they are noticing, and make suggestions for improvements. The rate of process development has really improved since they started doing that, even though they still don't have a lot of extra time.

LOUISE'S OBSERVATIONS ABOUT PROCESS DEVELOPMENT

"A year into our growth plan," said Louise, "it became clear that we needed to tighten up our production processes so we could continue to scale up. We wanted to be able to predict with accuracy how long projects would take and how production teams would interact with each other. We needed more consistency in our methods.

"Kate, my daughter, took on board the project of defining our processes with all the stages from sales, instructional design, and graphic design, to development. Together with the production team, she hammered many of these out.

"Over time, these have been continuously refined and improved for better efficiencies. Two years later, these processes are so thoroughly embedded with the team that if we stray from following them, production will be up in arms protesting that we are running inefficiently.

"As it turned out, this was a critical piece of work. Clarifying our processes had a much wider impact on our business than I could have ever imagined. It defined our costing methodology for proposals and we could predict with accuracy the timescales for each project and all its stages.

"It enabled us to better communicate with our clients about how we work with them systematically. This inspired confidence and ultimately resulted in more repeat business. Finally and importantly, it laid the foundation for us to take on much larger multi-module projects and deliver these powerfully for our clients, and profitably for us."

THE BENEFITS OF IMPROVED PROCESSES

With the improved processes and systematic design and delivery methods, the design and production people win, as it is easier to deliver stronger results for clients by focusing more on the creative aspects of design and development. This is more rewarding for them.

Clients win. They get stronger results in less time.

The salespeople win. It is easier for them to secure new clients and far more repeat work, as they are able to provide stronger results with more cost-effective pricing.

Everyone wins!

MANAGEMENT OPERATIONAL SUPPORT

"Michael, I discovered another myth, but only after the problem had been rectified. That was when we introduced weekly Debriefs into the management team," said Louise.

She went on. "I always thought that since I have great staff, they would just come to me and tell me if there were a problem. That just wasn't the case."

Myth: Since I have great staff, they will just come and tell me if there is a problem.

Even though Louise did and does have great staff, there was a wall as she described it. Her staff didn't just come and tell her when there was a problem. They didn't want to bother her if they felt she was busy (which she always was).

"Before we introduced regular, weekly, one-to-one meetings with each of the managers," said Louise, "I would meet on an ad-hoc basis with staff and I would gather information or form decisions based on this sporadic review."

Perspective Shift: Introduce written weekly debriefs and regular weekly meetings with all key staff.

"Debriefs have made it easy for managers to keep me in the loop on the issues within the company while they are still small and can be easily addressed," Louise said. "I also hear about the small victories within each department, and I can celebrate these with the staff as well."

The Debrief

The Debrief is a written review of past events, with the intent of learning from experience. Done by each manager on a weekly basis, this tool serves a number of functions. It gives the manager a chance to review and recap the week, and plan for the coming week. The categories are quite simple, but since the content is based on each particular manager's activities, the Debrief becomes a customized tool that is directly relevant for each person who completes one. The eight core categories of the Debrief are:

1. Facts - a summarized review of the main things that occurred during the week
2. Key accomplishments - big ones and little ones too
3. What worked or is working - specific things that may not have been accomplishments, but that were worth noting
4. What didn't work or isn't working - specific things that happened ... these get noted too
5. What's missing - allows for room to identify any structures, processes, and priorities that may need to be added
6. Opportunities - either already existing, or that have been uncovered with this debrief
7. Top three to five intended accomplishments for the coming week - brings focus to the week ahead
8. Anything else? - allows a space to acknowledge anything not caught above.

"Weekly debriefs have fundamentally changed the way we communicate in our business," said Louise. "They form a key structure, which enables us to better communicate with each other.

"Today, I have weekly meetings on a Monday with all my managers where they bring their debrief form and we discuss the past week, reflect on key achievements, what worked, and what hasn't. We then finish up with their key intended accomplishments for the coming week.

"I particularly listen for the positive things they are saying about other staff members so I can thank and acknowledge them. If there is an issue or problem, we can address it immediately. Debriefs have also been instrumental in enabling us to make small continuous improvements to processes and business systems that serve our clients better."

"Louise," I commented. "Weekly debriefing with each of the key people in a company can make such a huge difference, but it is a quiet and subtle tool. This is a support structure for increased communication. Otherwise, people are left with the feeling that they have to guess about issues they may not be experienced in resolving."

"Michael, it was only after introducing this tool that I realized just how much uncertainty there was among my key staff about so many issues. By having better information on what was happening weekly, I could weigh in while it was still early and help my people nip issues in the bud, while they were still small.

"This has saved my staff a lot of undue worry and stress, and has increased the productivity of every single department. Our communication with each other is much stronger because of the addition of that weekly structure."

PRODUCT DEVELOPMENT

"The company's product/service mix has continued to evolve as you have grown," I observed.

"Yes," agreed Louise. "However, much of this was in ways I didn't expect. I originally thought our product mix was fine, and that we needed to spend our time looking for ways to increase sales, instead of changing what was working."

> **Myth: Our product/service mix is fine the way it is. There are more important things to focus on, so leave this one alone.**

However, Kate felt differently.

"Kate has this fanatical commitment to client care," said Louise. "She wants to be proud of what we provide to our clients (we all do), but she takes it to a whole different level from most.

"She has been known to disrupt production processes, stopping things midstream to make changes. These changes sometimes cost us all of our profit on a job, but I must admit they were always really good 'catches' of things we should have thought of earlier."

"I know that Kate has been instrumental in the ongoing evolution of your product offering," I observed.

"Kate's position is clear," said Louise. "Innovative product development and evolution in a growing company is never finished."

> **Perspective Shift: Product development and evolution in a growing company is never finished.**

"I must admit," said Louise, "that our product offering is only as strong as it is due to Kate's consistent pushing on this. That's why now, as Creative Director of the company, she is in charge of all product evolution and continued improvement. She sees things that never occur to the rest of us, and her commitment has driven most major product changes we have implemented."

A New Learning Management System and the "Q"

Louise went on to explain how the "Q" decision-making tool

helped Kate implement a new Learning Management System (LMS).

"One example of this was the implementation of a new LMS. Kate took this on as a twelve-month project, and sure enough, it took all twelve months. However, even along the way, we hit snags and bumps that could have cost us additional time, forcing us to miss our deadlines for these types of initiatives. Kate used some of the tools she got in your training to keep things moving.

"When developing the new system, there were many instances where we felt stuck. We had an old system that needed to be rebuilt using new technologies and we needed to gain clarity on what needed to change and how and when we could do it.

"The project also would involve some serious investment of time and money.

"To help us envision where we were and where we wanted to go, Kate used the 'Q' in a team meeting. This helped us to think about the LMS in a structured way. Wasn't that your own tool, Michael?"

"Yes," I said. "It is a simple, but effective tool to help people gain clarity when moving forward on initiatives."

"Well, it worked," she replied, "and helped us to form the blueprint for moving forward on the project, which we went on to complete in twelve months.

"I have come to discover that getting stuck is often a result of jumbled thinking when facts, feelings, aspirations, and limitations all conspire to create blocks. This results in inaction and frustration.

"Kate's use of the 'Q' helped us clear the confusion and keep us on track. It allowed us to stop, step back, and 'reverse engineer' from our desired level of service to what it would take to get there, quickly and in a quantified manner. Her work on product evolution has generated significant results. We have better processes that are better documented. This, in turn, has led us to creating new jobs and eventually whole new departments."

The "Q"

The "Q" is a simple, yet effective, four-step decision-making tool that helps people clarify situations, sort out problems, and build effective strategies. The focus here is to have enough active thinking within a limited time on a number of aspects of any particular situation to gain clarity and be able to move forward productively. The name "Q" stands for Quantify, Qualify, Quick.

It has been said that 90 percent of the effective completion of any project lies in its formulation. The other 10 percent lies in its implementation. If this is true, then the mental efforts of formulation will bring us a long distance toward our goal. With the Q, we can get 90 percent of the job done with conceptualization ... just think of the possibilities!

Step 1: Where are we now?

In Step 1, we ask ourselves, "Where are we now?" Ninety percent of a project's completion lies in its formulation, and 55 to 60 percent of effective formulation lies in getting clear on where we are now. This step is critical, yet most often overlooked (or underutilized) based on the assumption that "I already know where I am."

Step 2: Where are we going?

In Step 2, we list in as much detail as possible the desired outcome(s). We list as many aspects of the desired results as we can think of. The clearer we are about the results that we want, the clearer we can become about the gap between Steps 1 and 2.

Step 3: How might we get there?

Step 3 is an edit-free brainstorming section where different possible alternatives to get from Step 1 (where we are now) to Step 2 (where we want to go) are explored. We list whatever comes to mind, and make sure not to edit out any ideas, even bizarre ones, as they may lead to good ideas.

Step 4: S.M.A.R.T. Actions

In Step 4, we list the first three to five actions we plan to take to move this initiative forward. S.M.A.R.T. is an acronym that stands for Specific, Measurable, Attainable, Realistic, and Timely. Instead of dealing with too many steps, by identifying the first three to five, we will get into appropriate action (the desired state) and leave ourselves flexibility to adjust, depending upon the results of those first few steps.

Other operational structures that were improved included the addition of key components, and the attendant staffing to enhance the service offering to clients of the company. This started with the addition of project managers, and most recently has been expanded to include dedicated learning solutions architects.

By unbundling what Louise and Kate were doing, the company was becoming more scalable.

Project Managers

Louise talked about the development of the role of project manager within the company.

"When we first started out," she said, "the salespeople—Kate and I—also project-managed. The problem was that when we were doing more sales, the project management ball got dropped or passed on to one of the production team members who were juggling their aspect of the delivery as well as project managing.

"As we worked on documenting our processes, it became clear that a PM role was needed and looking back this was a big step. Within eighteen months, project management became a department of six full-time staff with its own manager, Andrea."

Learning Solutions Architects

"Most recently," she continued, "as we began to win larger projects with more complex solutions, we realized that we needed a different role from that of instructional designer. Again, this came from Kate. We devised the role of Learning Solutions Architect, a person who takes a more strategic and long-term view of our clients' elearning solutions. They get involved at the early stages of a project and determine the creative learning approach.

"This leads to another myth I believed."

> **Myth: Product improvements will only cost us money and reduce our margins.**

Kate really took on product development and evolution. The biggest concern that she faced was the feeling that the company couldn't afford to go that extra mile for the customers. However, Kate was convinced that with documented processes, the customers could be shown what was involved, and they would be willing to fund things properly, to get a better result.

Kate was right. The company priced the modules in a manner that allowed Sponge to be properly funded for the work being done, while still being responsible to clients. She also worked with various people on the team to support increased documentation of processes to make things more predictable.

Alan, the head of the Developers team, created a cost calculator, to provide the salespeople with better estimates of what different components of training development cost, based upon different complexities required by clients.

> **Perspective Shift: Product improvements, if done right, can actually improve margins.**

The result was more consistent deliverables, stronger margins, and happier clients who have been coming back more often for more elearning modules. Surprised initially, Louise has come to appreciate the financial benefits of these improvements. Even though upfront they looked like costs, they quickly became cost-savers. They also made it easier to sell the solutions to clients with increased confidence.

ENHANCING YOUR OPERATIONAL PROCESSES

> **Misconception: The best place to learn how to enhance your operational processes is from within the industry.**

"Michael," commented Louise, "I always thought that the natural place to go to learn and evolve our operational structures was to look at the other companies in our industry. I thought that this was the only logical place to go, to see how we could improve. A recent trip changed my thinking on that completely.

"I discovered that you can learn about your own operational structures from any situation, anywhere."

Perspective Shift: You can learn about your own operational structures from any situation, anywhere.

"Okay," I said. "I'll bite. What did you learn, in an unexpected setting?"

"Michael, as you know, you have often gone on about having breaks and holidays. In fact, you regularly check in with me during our mentoring sessions to make sure I have them planned into my diary. The benefits of a break are obvious for all to see. I come back to work relaxed, refreshed, and clear-headed, ready to take on any challenges. But they also have another major benefit. I find that when I am away from work, whether taking the dog for a walk or going on holiday, new experiences bring about new ideas and ways of thinking from a fresh perspective. Even in the most unlikely places when Mark and I went on holiday and illness struck.

"After a ten-hour flight to Phoenix, my husband Mark complained of not feeling well and was getting a lot of discomfort from a leg ulcer he had. Rather than being a minor annoyance, it turned out to be a serious leg infection requiring an operation. We ended up having much of our holiday in the Tucson Medical Center. Fortunately, it worked out all right in the end, and he is okay now.

"The hospital visit made a big impression on me and I observed the way it worked that gave me ideas to introduce into the operational aspects of my business."

Louise went on to explain.

Whiteboards for sharing information easily

"While spending long hours in a hospital room," she said, "I started to notice certain things, like the big whiteboard in his room. The nurses would come in and write any vital information on Mark's health, his medicines, or diet to communicate quickly to the doctors and when nursing staff changed over.

"In British hospitals, patients have clipboards with notes attached to the base of their beds. I thought the big whiteboard was preferable as it was a quicker way to communicate important information. I thought this was a great idea for business too.

"When I returned to work, I ordered a couple of whiteboards on wheels to use in meetings. As people started to see how useful they were, we ordered some more and these boards started to multiply like rabbits. Now in every department you can see whiteboards being used. Employees use them for stand ups (our daily meeting ritual in many of the departments), in client meetings, during candidate interviews, for deadlines coming up, and for recording new sales wins. It means that at a quick glance, we all know what is going on and the information is shared easily.

"That [hospital's use of whiteboards] was one thing I noticed, but there was one other thing as well," she added. "This pointed to an operational structure we could use for the benefit of our clients."

Water in a plastic cup and good customer experience

"While Mark was having his operation," said Louise, "I stayed in a large waiting room that was staffed by volunteers. They were glad to answer my questions about what stage the operation was at. I sat down and started reading a paper when a volunteer came over and offered me a cold glass of water in a plastic cup. The volunteer must have sensed my concern and wanted to make a small kind gesture. I realized that it is the simple little things like this that you recall when you think of a good customer experience.

"It also made me reflect on how we need to look out for

and identify 'water in a plastic cup' moments—simple little things that clients will appreciate that add up to a memorable customer experience. We have built these into a part of our ongoing client care. Each staff person is empowered to find little things that would enrich our client's experience throughout the process. They are really enjoying making a difference with small, meaningful gestures."

"So Louise," I summarized, "you have improved your operational processes. Your management communication support and your products have continued to evolve as well," I said. "What's next?"

"Let's talk about our people," she said. "We have done lots there, and I have learned more than I ever expected."

"Sounds great!"

Summary of Myths and Misconceptions

1. Myth: People will naturally build the processes they need as they need them.
2. Myth: Since I have great staff, they will just come and tell me if there is a problem.
3. Myth: Our product/service mix is fine the way it is. There are more important things to focus on, so leave this one alone.
4. Myth: Product improvements will only cost us money and reduce our margins.
5. Misconception: The best place to learn how to enhance your operational processes is from within the industry.

Summary of Perspective Shifts

1. Process development requires active and consistent focus. Assign someone to be champion for process development.
2. Introduce written weekly debriefs and regular weekly meetings with all key staff.
3. Product development and evolution in a growing company is never finished.
4. Product improvements, if done right, can actually improve margins.
5. You can learn about your own operational structures from any situation, anywhere.

Tools Introduced in this Chapter

1. The Weekly Debrief
   a. Facts
   b. Key Accomplishments
   c. What worked or is working
   d. What didn't work or isn't working
   e. What's missing
   f. Opportunities
   g. Top three to five intended accomplishments for next week
   h. Anything else?
2. The "Q"
   a. Where are we now?
   b. Where are we going?
   c. How might we get there?
   d. S.M.A.R.T. Actions

Section 2: People

"Great vision without great people is irrelevant."
Jim Collins, Best-selling author of *Good to Great*

7 CORPORATE CULTURE

"Core values don't just define our internal culture, but also [define] the clients we work with and the suppliers we choose. They have a far-reaching impact."
Louise Pasterfield, Managing Director, Sponge UK

EVOLVING THE CORPORATE CULTURE

Corporate culture has a large impact on any company. Whether we pay conscious attention to this or not, a culture will form within any organization. If it's not the one we set, it will be the one that shows up by default.

When we began the review of the progress that Sponge has made over the past three years, I asked Louise to reflect on how her evolving role within the company affected Sponge's corporate culture.

"I think as I started to view the business from a bigger perspective and more strategically, the more the staff's trust and confidence has grown," said Louise. "This shift in my role has been one of a number of things that has affected the evolution of our company culture.

"It is interesting to observe that, although I never really considered it at the time, all the staff used to feed off my energy. If I was in good shape, everyone seemed happy. If I was panicked about some deadline or stressed about money, my people would pick that up and it would affect them as well. They fed off my mood as their boss. I think they still do, even though we are much larger than we were."

One key element in consciously setting (or resetting) our corporate culture is uncovering and actively working with the company's core values.

The Gallup organization has completed a number of long-term studies on company performance and employee engagement, and their links to the development and maintenance of a company's corporate culture.

I recall at a Vancouver Board of Trade speech several years ago, Brad Anderson, CEO of Best Buy at the time, recounting the findings of one of Gallup's studies. He said a study found that the company with the strongest corporate culture in the United States was Best Buy, the consumer electronics giant. They also found that the company with the most dismal corporate culture was—you guessed it—Best Buy!

How could this be? This makes no sense, until you dig a little further and realize that a company has as many corporate cultures as it has managers. Each manager has his or her own set of guiding principles by which s/he operates. This accounts for much of the difference. Unless there is an overriding set of guiding principles to which everyone adheres, this phenomenon will occur time after time.

When I met Louise three years ago, her company had a staff of ten (including Louise) and she was the only manager. Everything operated from her personal guiding principles. I knew that as the company grew, this would need conscious attention, or else Louise would be plagued with many of the same frustrations that most growing companies routinely encounter—communication problems and divided self-interests of a growing, and increasingly difficult-to-manage staff.

Managing People is Like Herding Cats

We have all heard the saying that *managing people is like herding cats*. You feel like you are chasing them, as they go off in all directions. The word "hopeless" comes to mind.

However, there is a way to herd cats. Yes, it is quite simple. All you need to do is to get out in front of them with a tin of catnip, and they will quickly follow you wherever you go. Any cat owner who uses an electric can-opener as part of the feeding process will immediately resonate with this notion. Just hit the button on the can-opener and with that unique sound, the family cat comes running, in anticipation.

The Key Question

How do you take a group of people with diverse backgrounds and very different levels of skill, experience, and business knowledge, and get them all working from the same page?
1. Identify the page that you want everyone to work from. For people, the equivalent to catnip is your Vision and your Core Values (or guiding principles).
   Remember, Vision has that incredibly fast, limbic energy, and people will get excited and follow a leader with a compelling vision.
2. Only work with people who want to work from the same page as you. This is your brand or flavor of catnip. Instead of trying to change people, let them choose.
3. Develop and implement structures to create and nurture an environment where that page becomes "natural" to everyone.

Yet, too often, people in business treat Vision and Values as nice to have, but really kind of "touchy-feely," not the substance of solid business growth, and definitely not practical on a day-to-day basis.

Louise was of that belief as well.

CORE VALUES

In spite of Louise's previous belief about the "value" of identifying Core Values, she did identify and entrench a solid set of six core values into her company's culture that her staff understand, support, and act upon on a daily basis.

The Core Values of Sponge UK
1. Act with integrity
2. Bring a commitment to excellence
3. Focus on clients
4. Be accountable
5. Commit to the team
6. Inspire confidence

However, in order to get there, Louise had to address some significant myths and misconceptions she had before realizing a meaningful perspective change.

> **Myth: Core values don't impact the day-to-day running of the business.**

"I must admit, Michael," said Louise, "that initially, when you suggested we develop core values, I thought it was a good idea, but at the back of mind I was slightly cynical.

"It brought to mind a time when I visited a large company that boldly displayed their values in their reception area (based on excellent customer service), when in reality I knew from research that many of their customers weren't that happy.

"Part of me felt that this would be one of those nice-to-have things, but not useful on a day-to-day basis, and definitely not as critical as they turned out to be."

Intrigued by Louise's comments, I dug a bit deeper.

"We uncovered those in our first series of meetings together, as part of my initial visit, three years ago. When did you change your mind about their value?" I asked.

About this, she was quite clear.

"The benefit of the core values internally revealed themselves when we had a staff problem," explained Louise. "One of our values is to 'Commit to team' as all our projects require working collaboratively with each other.

"This means, for example, handing over your aspect of the project such as storyboards as thoroughly and completely as you can to the design and development teams. This, in turn, helps them do their jobs more effectively and ensures the success of the project as a whole.

"In this instance, one staff member, Myron [not his real name], rarely would provide a clean handover. Instead, he blamed the other teams when there were issues down the line and created a feeling of alienation between departments.

"Despite numerous discussions with Myron, the problem kept coming up and I would hear about it during my weekly debriefs with most of the other managers. This was having a caustic effect in production and it was clear that this person had to go.

> **Perspective Shift: Core values are a critical part of building an effective and collaborative staff team.**

"He lasted less than twelve months with us and I realize now, it was an expensive way to learn that core values matter. Had I used the values as you initially suggested in our recruiting efforts, Myron would have never made it through our doors."

Myth: Core values are just an internal tool.

The key to having core values operate so effectively is to ensure that the values identified are not just aspirations … something we strive for. Instead, they must be showstoppers.

What are those things that, if they are not adhered to, can hurt the company? And what are those things that if done well would not only benefit the company, but your employees and customers as well?

The reason that many people's core values are not as effective is that they have not been set up as showstoppers. Unless you would fire someone for violating a core value, it is not a core value.

If core values are set up with this standard in mind, then they are incredibly useful.

"As you know, Michael," said Louise, "we did identify our core values as inviolable. After the experience with Myron, we built questions into our recruitment process to ask all prospective candidates to ensure that everyone we hired aligned with our culture.

"Periodically we still run into problems. Someone who shouldn't be part of our team slips through, but we are usually able to eliminate anyone who is not a fit before hiring them, using the values as one of our screening tools."

> **Perspective Shift: Core values can also support our efforts to define the clients we work with and the suppliers we choose.**

Used properly, core values can really become the guiding light for the entire organization. They are not just an internal tool, but also a set of principles that generate the rules that people follow, both within and beyond the confines of the company.

People use core values to guide selection of their suppliers, their customers, and colleagues as well.

Initially, after that experience with Myron, the employee who didn't fit, Louise thought that core values were a powerful internal tool, but she was still not convinced that they were of any use externally. After all, she was still thinking of the company that claimed in their values to be committed to strong customer service, when in reality that was not what their customers experienced.

Then she gained a shift in perspective, based on a client incident.

Louise recalled, "We had an incident with a client we had been working with for a couple of years. At the time, they represented approximately 10 percent of our turnover. Acting with integrity is one of our core values, and an event occurred that clearly called into question the client's honesty. I heard about the problem during weekly debriefs from every manager. It resulted in project teams becoming demotivated and not enjoying working on that client's projects.

"I knew what I needed to do. On Monday morning, I rang the client and politely and respectfully told them that we no longer wanted to work together."

"How did it feel, making that call?" I asked.

"I was nervous," she admitted. "It felt good to stick with our values, and it felt great to back up my staff. But I was still worried.

"It was a bold move financially to give up 10 percent of our turnover. But as it turned out, it freed us up to work on other projects we enjoyed more, with clients who had similar values to ours.

"Surprisingly, it made no difference to our turnover. That year we grew by 80 percent."

Louise described the "value" of Core Values perfectly when she said, "I learned that core values don't just define our internal culture but also the clients we work with and the suppliers we choose. They have a far-reaching impact."

The people at Sponge really embrace the core values as their fundamental operating principles. They participate in exercises periodically to keep these present in the hearts and minds of all who work there. What follows is a sampling of some of the staff members' interpretations of what each of the six core values means to them.

1) Act with integrity

Alan: "To me acting with integrity is being honest with the client and providing the best advice and direction in any given circumstance. Working with a company of people who all share this core value enables us to have trust and confidence that we are all working to the same common goals and have the interest of the client at heart."

Carly: "If we don't always know the answer, we aren't afraid to admit it. Instead, we embrace the fact that learning is a journey that has no pre-defined end."

2) Bring a commitment to excellence

Kate: "Quite a big part of my job is judging whether what is being sent out of the business—from visuals to pitch presentations to proposal writing to storyboards—is good enough to be proud that it came from Sponge. It can be a difficult call to look at something and make changes when someone has clearly worked so hard on it and it also makes more work for me! But I'm reassured when I see it pay off.

"I know that my personal commitment to excellence, for example striving to think concepts through completely, critically analyzing my own solutions, communicating ideas clearly and in a compelling way, and even aiming to spell things correctly in my own work, helps us win new clients. And I know I fall short sometimes! But I always have that standard in mind to aim for."

Rhea S: "Because all our elearning is bespoke, we create elearning that is specifically designed to solve our clients' performance problems and achieve real results for them. I think our clients appreciate how we try to really understand what they need and create something that's completely unique to their business."

3) Focus on clients

Jason: "To me, this means having a real commitment to our delivery of bespoke solutions, ensuring the client is provided with excellent modules that satisfy their learning objectives and exceed their expectations. We constantly seek to provide clients with open channels of communication to all departments, to ensure they are able to have any queries or issues dealt with swiftly and efficiently."

Stephen: "We ensure the work that is sent off prior to being viewed by the client for the first time is checked by the developer, the lead developer, graphic design, and instructional design. We then account for two waves of amends by the client to ensure the finished product is exactly what they want. After all these processes have run, we are often left with a highly refined product."

4) Be accountable

Dan: "Customers stay loyal and collaborative when they trust your communications and are confident that you have their best interests at heart."

Glen: "We are always looking to do the very best for every client, making sure the work is totally based on the client's brief and needs—custom-made and absorbing."

5) Commit to the team

Jamie: "We ensure that team members have access to help when needed and make sure they don't feel alone in dealing with problems when they arise."

Rachel: "We are always happy to help other colleagues and recognize when times become stressful so that we can all pull together as a team! We generate the feeling of never having to deal with a difficult situation or client alone—everyone pulls together and a solution is always found."

6) Inspire confidence

Emma: "Telling people when they do a good job. Encouraging them. Sharing good news stories with everyone in the organization. Providing training to build new skills."

Jon: "Truthfulness will always inspire confidence. I will always have more faith in what a person is telling me (even if it is not what I want to hear) if they are known to be honest."

Developing the Company's Vision

Many people are confused about exactly what a company's vision really is. It could be best described as the answer to these questions:

1. Money aside, how do you want your business to make a difference?
2. Again, money aside, if this business were to evolve over the next ten to thirty years, how would you like to see it evolve?

Many people confuse this area with specific goals and objectives, or targets for increased growth and profit. Financial profit to a business is like eating is to life. There is far more to life than eating ... unless we are starving! Then we will spend much if not all of our focus on getting fed. Thankfully, for most of us, getting food is not a problem.

Financial profit for a business is just like that. If we do not have financial profit, we do not have a business. Yet there is so much more available from a business other than just the profit. It could be freedom. It could be some kind of contribution. It could be market (or world) dominance! There is no right answer.

The purpose of a company's vision is to capture exactly what that is for the owner(s) of a business. Then the people who are interested in that vision will be attracted to come and participate.

"How have you worked with your overall vision in the development of your company culture?" I asked Louise.

"Well, I wouldn't say that I have consciously used it, until quite recently," she said. "To me, a Vision has always been this larger-than-life statement that looks good on a wall, but has little to do with a company's daily operations. I always felt we didn't need that for us."

> **Myth: A company vision is a larger-than-life goal that hangs on a wall, but has little to do with the company's daily operations.**

"I would suggest to you, Louise, that this is exactly what a Vision is, when it is not working. Notice that even though you didn't formally acknowledge your Vision, you still were operating with one," I pointed out.

She reflected on this.

"We didn't call it a Vision, but as a company we were united in competing with 'The Big Guys' in our industry. We have always been out to prove that we were just as effective as our larger competitors. We have done a great job in generating a high level of credibility within our market."

Louise added, "However, things are changing very quickly.

"With the influx of additional staff, I am noticing the need to articulate our vision and direction for the company. We are no longer considered a baby among giants, but a credible company in our own right. We have won awards for the caliber of our work.

"New people are not joining a little company. They now perceive us as a strong and growing business, and they are hitching their destiny to this rising star. And everyone is asking me where we are headed ... what's our Vision?"

> **Perspective Shift: A Vision is a meaningful statement about either where we are headed, or what the company is all about ... its essence.**

Not all Visions have to be about some future destination. Starbucks Coffee has tens of thousands of locations, yet their Vision is about the experience and environment each individual location contributes to the people who visit—that bistro feel that supports people within community. It is not about size of organization at all.

Louise commented, "I found the conversation you and I had, Michael, about vision, to make it a lot easier than I expected it to be. Rather than some larger-than-life statement, you just asked me what I loved about the business and our growth plans."

And with that, she shared with me her vision for Sponge UK.

"To me, the company is a place where I am constantly challenged to learn and grow. I have learned more about operating a business in the past three years, than I have all my adult life. I find it very exciting. And when you told me recently that I would learn even more this coming year than I had during those past three years, I found that even more exciting.

"Every day has challenges; yet, with each of these, I am learning new things constantly. I have never been so fulfilled in my work as I am now.

"Also, for our staff, our growth really pushes them to learn as well. At times, it is not easy. But it's really rewarding to see people accomplish things and to grow into new roles. I love being able to contribute to their growth and development, and their sense of satisfaction of what they are able to achieve for our clients, and each other.

"And the best part of all this is that we are doing this learning and growing, while providing tools for our clients to learn and grow as well.

"So our vision is all about learning and creating an environment for learning and growth, for me, for my people and for our clients."

I paused, to let this absorb, then said.

"Do you know, Louise, that some people would call that a lofty Vision? However, the way you describe it, this is clearly meaningful to you. As a result, it is very compelling. Visions don't have to be lofty. They do have to be meaningful, and yours is, very much so."

"Anything else about your corporate culture to review?"

"I'm sure we could talk about lots, but let's move on," said Louise.

"Okay," I said. "Now let's look at what has shifted for you in hiring."

Summary of Myths and Misconceptions

1. Myth: Core values don't impact the day-to-day running of the business.
2. Myth: Core values are just an internal tool.
3. Misconception: A company vision is a larger-than-life goal that hangs on a wall, but has little to do with the company's daily operations.

Summary of Perspective Shifts

1. Core values are a critical part of building an effective and collaborative staff team.
2. Core values can also support our efforts to define the clients we work with and the suppliers we choose.
3. A Vision is a meaningful statement about either where we are headed, or what the company is all about ... its essence.

8 HIRING - PART 1

"No matter how brilliant your mind or strategy, if you're playing a solo game, you'll always lose out to a team."
Reid Hoffman, LinkedIn Co-founder

One of the most important aspects of growing a business is the process of hiring new people into a company. Nearly every business owner will tell you that it is hard to find great people. Great people are just not out there! They are happily working for someone else. Are there that few great people out there? Or is there more to the process of recruiting and selecting top-notch people than meets the eye?

Statistics fly around constantly about the cost of bad hires. I have heard estimates that the cost of hiring the wrong people is anywhere from three to ten times someone's salary. This added cost may include anything from missed sales opportunities to strained customer and employee relations, potential legal issues, and resources to hire and train candidates.

Regardless of the exact number, most people agree that the cost of poor hiring decisions is at least tens of thousands, if not one hundred thousand or more (whether that is in dollars, pounds, or yen). Hiring mistakes are expensive to any business, let alone a small to medium-sized company with limited capital.

There is much talk these days about hiring A-Players. Originally a term from sport—the premier players were on the A-Squad, while the next level were the Bs, and so on—this term was made popular in North America when it was used as the title of the 1983 TV Action series, *The A-Team*, with George Peppard. The A-Team was a group of four ex-USA military with extraordinary individual abilities.

The term was picked up and refined by Brad Smart in his breakthrough hiring process called *Topgrading*.[4] The term has become very commonly used and is referred to by many consultants and hiring experts, referring to A-Players as a company's top tier of personnel—in other words, great people.

Using Brad Smart's perspective, a "Topgrading" company hires only A-Players—those who would qualify as being the top 10 percent of all people who would fit a certain role for comparable pay. Smart referenced B-Players as those who constitute the next 25 percent (from the 66th percentile to the 90th percentile) and C-Players as the bottom 65 percent of the people who would be eligible for this job at comparable pay. Brad Smart's advice, as well as the advice of many, is to hire only A-Players for our companies, in order to achieve maximum results.[5]

In a growing company, hiring A-Players becomes even more critical. I have found over the years that unless we are hiring A-Players, growing a company will be much harder, if not impossible to achieve.

Anyone who has had one or more real stars on their team who also fit the company's culture will be able to attest to the following: One *great* person in your company can be as valuable

[4]Smart, Bradford D. *Topgrading, 3rd Edition: The Proven Hiring and Promoting Method That Turbocharges Company Performance*. New York, NY: Portfolio/Penguin, 2012.
[5]Ibid.

as three *good* people. A positive, resourceful, and giving person who anticipates what's needed, and provides it just as it is needed, will save us time, money, stress, and heartache. It is truly a gift to have such a person on the team.

What if the whole company were populated with people like that? Wouldn't it be amazing? Actually, it is necessary to load the team with these people if we want to maximize our goals for effective growth, profit, and freedom.

To hire only A-Players sounds like good advice and it is! However, it is so general that it is not useful. After all, is there anyone who wants to hire second-rate employees? The concern is that most business owners, while good or even great at producing and/or delivering products and services, are not great at attracting and hiring top-notch people.

In short, we don't know how.

THE STRUGGLES OF HIRING THE "RIGHT-FIT" STAFF

Louise faced many challenges finding the right staff for her company as it grew. Remember that she grew from a staff of ten people in June 2011—comprising of herself, her daughter Kate, the part-time accountant Matt, and seven other staff members—to twenty-nine people three years later.

"As we began to grow," said Louise, "we started to take on more staff. We would write up a job description, which basically was a list of bullets broken down into 'must have' and 'be good to have.'

"Because we were busy, we didn't spend a long time exploring different places where we could advertise a vacancy. We were often disappointed with the quality and number of candidates for a position. We would choose the best of the bunch because we were under pressure to fill the vacancy. Sometimes this worked out and sometimes it didn't.

"We were also careful to keep salaries as low as possible to keep overheads down, which often meant taking on more junior people.

"As we grew, we found it hard to find the staff we needed, in particular, instructional designers and developers.

"We are based in Plymouth, a city of approximately 250,000 people on the South West Coast of England. Plymouth is about 3.5 hours outside London. In London, it is easier to recruit because there is a much larger pool of people in the big city.

"Initially, this seemed like an insurmountable problem. Did we need to open a London office if we couldn't find people in Plymouth? I found that we were becoming so stuck on the problem and the story we were telling ourselves that it was blocking our thoughts on exploring all the possibilities of solving it. Looking back, I think we were talking ourselves into this limitation."

There are two parts to hiring people. Those are

- Selection - choosing the "right-fit" person from a pool of candidates
- Recruiting - developing a deep enough pool of talent from which to choose candidates

Louise needed to work on both.

THE SELECTION PROCESS

In her efforts to hire the people she needed—the "right-fit" candidates—Louise was being held back by some common myths about hiring in a growing business. But as she and I reviewed these myths, Louise had some major perspective shifts.

> **Myth: When hiring, take the best of the bunch and get on with it. They are obviously all that are available to choose from.**

> **Myth: Most people won't be as good as you, so don't spend too much time looking. You might just be disappointed anyway.**

> **Myth: Always take on less expensive people to protect the company's profit.**

"Before we had a formal process, employee selection was hit and miss," explained Louise. "We took on people who were the best of the bunch but not necessarily the best for the job. After all, we thought, someone who could do part of the job was better than nobody at all. Or we took on a person because we needed someone to fill a job quickly. Or we took them because they weren't that expensive."

> **Perspective Shift: Less expensive people may cost you more money in the long run.**

"One of the most uncomfortable moments," said Louise, "was when you said that we would most likely have to pay a lot more for really good A-Players. As a small business owner, my thinking was to keep wage costs down as low as possible."

"Yet you followed the advice," I commented.

"Yes," she said, "well what you had said up until that point was all working out, one way or another, so I thought to myself, 'I'm not paying this man to disregard his advice, and my way doesn't seem to be working, so let's give it a go.'"

"My perspective changed as we began to hire A-Players. Having these higher talented, and yes, more expensive people on the team meant that I had to do far less on projects. They got the job done better, and also freed me up to work on growing the business."

"It sounds like it worked out pretty well for you," I said.

"It started working much better when you taught me how to hire correctly, but it did take some practice as it was a new way of working," she asserted. "Since then, we have done much better."

> **Perspective Shift: When hiring, you *can* get what you want. Get clear on what you want, in writing.**

> **Perspective Shift: Follow an established and effective hiring protocol.**

INTRODUCTION OF A SELECTION PROCESS: LOUISE'S REVIEW

One of the first things I did with Louise when she started working with us was to provide training in the selection of employees. I knew that she was going to be uncomfortable with this. But Louise needed to spend more to hire senior people in order to free Kate and herself up to do other things.

Louise also had to explore more recruitment options so she could get as many good CVs as possible. For Sponge, located in the southwest of the UK, this meant also using recruitment agencies. I warned Louise that this may take time, and not to just take someone on because they were okay.

Louise commented, "I found that hard. There were pressures

on me, on Kate, and on our other people. I wanted to relieve the pressure, but I knew you were probably right when you said that I would only suffer in the long run if I 'settled' for someone just to fill the vacancy. We stayed the course, and while it was uncomfortable at the start, it has been paying off dramatically."

GETTING CLEAR ON WHAT WE WANT – IN WRITING

One of the most common mistakes people make when hiring is to make assumptions about the role to be filled, rather than committing all the relevant details to writing. Here is an example of the process that Louise followed, that supported her in gaining stronger staff.

"We were hiring for a senior Instructional Designer (ID) at the time," said Louise. "The first place we started was with the Job Chunks and Duties. This was much more detailed information than the job descriptions we were using. After writing out the purpose of this role, we broke the job down into three to five main job chunks—the main categories of responsibility within the role—and then detailed in writing all the duties and responsibilities that related to each chunk.

"After that, we wrote specific and general attributes to support these. Although it sounds like a simple task, the first few took me hours to do. I found it easier to think about the responsibilities in terms of the order that tasks get done to achieve the results within a particular job chunk, and this helped me figure that piece out.

"To all this, we added the attributes from our six core values. There were a few instances when some new staff could do their jobs, but just weren't a good fit with the company. We learned the lesson to include this piece after our experience with Myron, a senior ID we hired who didn't fit the culture.

"Then came the ad we would place in a number of different

online directories. This ad, rather than a listing of duties and skills, was written in more of a short paragraph format with a bit of flair. We found it so much more compelling for our potential candidates, to generate their interest if we shared the emotional excitement we have here at the office. Lists just don't convey that, but we found that a plain, paragraph-format ad could be written to generate far more interest."

PREPARING FOR THE SELECTION PROCESS

Preparation plays an integral role in the selection process. No matter how well we might do, just asking questions as they occur to us, we do a far more effective job of gaining the information we need if we have taken the time to prepare. With the high cost of mis-hires, it only makes sense to invest the time to ensure we have the highest possible chance of sorting between best-fit and near-miss candidates.

Louise has taught her team to take the time to prepare properly for each phase of the selection process.

"First we clarified the job, and exactly what we were looking for in terms of each candidate's skills and fit with the company," said Louise. "Then we worked on telephone interview sheets so we could ask potential applicants questions that directly related to the duties and responsibilities we identified, and both the skills they would need to do their job and the attributes that supported their fit with the company.

"This was followed by face-to-face interview questions, which we also prepared in advance. Then we added in a test that was particular to their role, and if they did well at this, they came in for a second interview. It became a robust and well-documented selection process to ensure that we took on the best people.

"With a formal process, we slowed the whole thing down. We took the time to find as many candidates as we could.

We started to look ahead to forecast our staffing needs so we weren't hiring in a panic. We focused on A-Players, even if they were more expensive.

"One thing I really like about having a set process in place is that managers are now using the same templates and systems to hire staff. We all use the same telephone interview question templates and face-to-face questions, and have included tests (depending on their job role) that candidates all have to answer if they are successful at the first interview. As part of the selection process, we have embedded questions on core values to ensure they are a good fit with our company, not just with the job.

"What's interesting now is that my managers are really listening for evidence that candidates fit in with our core values. Just yesterday, when I asked one of my managers how they got on with an interview, she said, 'I am sure the candidate could definitely do the job, but you know they just weren't the right cultural fit so we won't be taking it further.'

"As a result of these processes, our retention of staff is high. Taking more time to define the role in writing, recruiting far and wide, and being more selective in whom we take on has really paid off dramatically.

"Successful candidates have said that it has been one of the toughest hiring processes they have been through. But at least when people join, we are confident that they are a good fit and are likely to stay. In fact, some of the people who have joined our team have done so, in part, because the hiring process was so rigorous. They said that if we care that much about who gets into our company, it must be a great place to work!"

THE CHALLENGES OF RECRUITING

Louise and her team are now better at selecting people who are the right fit for the company. Yet, there are two sides to hiring.

The other side is recruiting—sourcing and developing an adequate pool of talent from which to choose the best-fit staff.

Louise had described the selection side, but what about the recruiting side. What were Louise's experiences growing the pool of potential applicants? I asked Louise if she had any difficulties recruiting strong applicants.

"Yes," said Louise, "it could be difficult recruiting people in Plymouth, but there were talented people out there and we just needed to start looking in different places. Getting to be as clear as we were was half the battle. Then we expanded our search beyond the traditional ads that were online, in the paper, and on our website.

"The first place we started to make progress was through people we knew. Kate had a contact with someone in a TV production company who led us to taking on Andrea, our first Project Manager.

"Andrea knew people she worked with: Carly, Rachel, and Chris. Carly and Rachel joined the project management team, and Chris joined us as an LMS developer .

"James, one of our instructional designers knew Katie, an ex-teacher who joined us as an instructional designer trainee. In most departments, the team has grown through people they know. Since we knew them, we didn't go after anyone we didn't think would fit with us.

"We also took on university placement students like Jon. If they were good (like Jon was), we promised them a job after graduation. Jon helped us find two other developers who were graduates in his year.

"This year, we will attend a recruitment fair at the University to attract more graduates. Presently, 40 percent of our staff are University of Plymouth graduates.

"We originally tried to avoid recruitment agencies because of the high fees, but in reality, they were necessary. We learned which ones were the good ones, who properly screened candidates before sending through CVs.

"Also, we found what each of the firms' relative strengths were; so for example, some were excellent at finding salespeople but not developers. With that information, we could save time by working with them at their point of strength and find other recruiters who were good with finding different types of people.

"Presently, we are experimenting with Executive Search services to find a Head of Instructional Design.

"We also have experimented with more advertising online. That's where we recruited Emma, our Marketing Manager. Recently, Alex our head of Graphic Design has been using LinkedIn extensively. So far, he has been successful in finding many promising candidates.

"As we have grown, I find that more potential candidates are seeking us out. These are usually people who are looking to relocate to the South West and have found us on Google. After we rebranded and improved our website, we noticed more CVs coming through that vehicle as well."

Louise summarized. "It has been truly amazing. There is so much that I have learned that I didn't realize I didn't know. And the results are very different now than they were three years ago."

"So, what has shifted in your thinking in this area?" I asked.

Louise thought for a moment before responding.

"I have come to the realization," she said, "that recruitment is really a marketing exercise. We need to be where potential candidates are when they decide to look for a job. Currently, we are creating a brochure about what it is like to work at Sponge, in order to attract more candidates.

"We are on a recruitment drive right now for twenty-one new staff. That will bring our total staff count to fifty people, and that is in addition to our group of freelancers. I have decided to take on an in-house recruiter, Tifenn, who is helping coordinate all our activities. With so much going on, she has been making a real difference already.

"What else have you learned about hiring as it relates to growing a business?" I asked, suspecting that there was more.

"I have finally decided to accept your suggestion to hire 'ahead of the curve.'"

Myth: When growing a business, add people only as sales demands require. Lead with sales, then get the people as needed.

"My perspectives on all this are now quite different," she said and went on to explain this shift in perspective that she experienced.

Perspective Shift: Hire "ahead of the curve."

"Hiring 'ahead of the curve,'" Louise said, "has been one of the single most difficult concepts to get my head around as a business owner. Why would I spend money before I have to?

"At the moment, we are in the midst of our recruitment drive to hire twenty-one people. I have found this very challenging. But I know if we don't do it, we won't be able to maintain our growth.

"Hiring at the last minute, just before you need people is usually expensive. It also reduces the candidate pool, because of the condensed timeframes.

"The idea of hiring ahead of the curve is a bit like buying a plane ticket. You don't like having to pay in advance but if you book earlier, the cheaper it will be. Leaving it to the last minute usually means more expensive tickets and less choice."

"That's a great analogy," I said.

"Our managers have had a difficult time with this idea. They think, what will the new employees do if they aren't that busy when they start? I have found though, that new starters take a few months to get fully up to speed and be productive. This strategy gives them a chance to settle in and have a proper induction rather than being thrown in the deep end to learn the hard way.

"The results we have seen so far are incredible. People are better trained for their jobs, and productivity gets very high, very quickly. The other people in the department also feel much better supported with an extra person or two supporting them while learning our systems, rather than always feeling behind client commitments and deadlines due to staff shortages or needing to help untrained, new staff. That's a very different reality for everyone."

We all know that it can be difficult to recruit and select great people for our companies as we grow. What Louise discovered was that by treating this part of business growth as critical, she and her team have been doing what it takes to maximize their effectiveness through the use of proven and documented processes. As a result, they have been able to dramatically improve their hiring results. That is making all the difference in the world to the task of growing this business to a whole new level.

Summary of Myths and Misconceptions

1. Myth: When hiring, take the best of the bunch and get on with it. They are obviously all that are available to choose from.
2. Myth: Most people won't be as good as you, so don't spend too much time looking. You might just be disappointed anyway.
3. Myth: Always take on less expensive people to protect the company's profit.
4. Myth: When growing a business, add people only as sales demands require. Lead with sales, then get the people as needed.

Summary of Perspective Shifts

1. Less expensive people may cost you more money in the long run.
2. When hiring, you *can* get what you want. Get clear on what you want in writing.
3. Follow an established and effective hiring protocol.
4. Hire "ahead of the curve."

9 HIRING – PART 2

"First-rate people hire first-rate people; second-rate people hire third-rate people."
Leo Rosten

As Louise and I continued the three-year review, we discovered other myths and misconceptions she had encountered and ultimately overcome in the process of refining her hiring process. These fell into three distinct, but related, areas:

1. difficulties in hiring A-Players as employees
2. choosing the right people to be managers
3. selecting titles for employees

All three of these areas generally impact companies on their path of growth. Sponge was no exception.

One very common trap for managers to get caught up in, especially as a company is preparing for large-scale growth, is to hire people who are junior, rather than getting more talented help. Many feel threatened by hiring top talent, concerned that the manager will lose his/her job to the new recruit.

"If I hire this high calibre team member, what will I do?" is a very common response that I see with employees who don't understand the growth that is coming, or who feel uncertain in their own skills, and as a result, feel insecure and threatened about their evolving role in the company.

"This myth is not mine," said Louise, "but I have definitely seen this with a couple of our newer managers."

DIFFICULTIES IN HIRING A-PLAYERS AS EMPLOYEES

> **Myth: As a manager, never hire someone who is better than you. They could take your job.**

Louise explained.

"From my perspective, I thought this was a non-issue. Surely, people would know that we intend to help them grow into larger roles as we grow, and that they need to free themselves up to be available to take on more responsibility. However, a couple of the junior managers who didn't comprehend the bigger picture would try to hire only inexperienced staff.

"When asked, the response I would get back was, 'I don't really need someone stronger than this person. She will be fine. That's all I need. Let's not waste money.' Of course, what they were also doing was protecting their current role, making sure there were things for them to do.

"And while I knew that I would need them in a larger capacity, unless I could point to specific tasks I wanted done at a more senior level—enough of those to fill a full-time role—they would agree with me to my face and then keep trying to hire junior people anyway.

"This really helped me understand better where each manager was in his or her development. As people face growth, anything that triggers them will show up. I am finding out lots about people's fears and self-imposed limitations as I work through all this."

"We all have fears," I said. "It is interesting to see what each person's fears look like. The more you can tell exactly what stops a person, the more you can provide specific support to help them move past their blocks so they can grow beyond them."

Louise smiled, for she realized that this was exactly what I was doing with her.

"This really takes a lot of patience," she said. "Sometimes I just want to get on with it. Then I have to stop myself, because I know that each person's growth is just as important as anything else we are doing here.

"The perspective shift I am trying to teach my staff is that if you cannot be replaced, you cannot be promoted."

Perspective Shift: If you cannot be replaced, you cannot be promoted.

As managers grow in their responsibilities, they usually need to delegate many—or all—of their previous tasks to others. Managing a group of eight to ten people is a full-time job in itself. Yet, if emerging managers treat the tasks they do as their measurable contribution, they may not realize that shedding those tasks is what will free them up to manage the larger department or functional area.

Louise commented on this.

"Pointing this out to people has really helped, but it can be a difficult idea to get your head around. Sometimes, for staff moving up into management, their future role may be harder to predict and I am not always able to clearly articulate enough detail of what their future role will entail. So I can understand their feelings of concern."

"Some people just take a bit longer than others," I commented. "In the end, it will all work out."

"That may be true," she agreed, "and leads me to another myth I discovered that in the past caused me some undue stress."

Myth: The people who are best at their jobs make the best managers.

It is fascinating how many people will take the person who is performing best at their current job within a growing department and make that person the manager. Most employees strive for this, as it signifies movement and growth in their career. The fact that an employee may not be well suited for management is completely overlooked by bosses and employees alike.

On the surface, promoting the best person makes sense from the employer's perspective. If we can trust someone to generate a result, chances are that this person can be trusted as a manager, right? Quite often, these people are the most enthusiastically engaged in the business as well.

What's More Important: Talent or Engagement?

A Gallup study with retail stores was designed to determine which is more important to organizational success—talent (skills for the job) or engagement.[6] They measured the impact of talent of store managers and the engagement of store managers against their relative impact on store performance.

Using low talent and disengaged managers as the baseline, if managers were highly talented yet still disengaged, they found that store performance was, on average, 11.8 percent higher than with low-talent, disengaged employees.

---

[6] Herway, Jake and Nate Dvorak. "What's More Important – Talent or Engagement?" *Gallup Business Journal*, April 22, 2014. Available online at: www.gallup.com/businessjournal/167708/important-talent-engagement.aspx.

Where managers were both talented and engaged, average store performance was 23.5 percent higher than the baseline level. Both of these results were to be expected.

However, where store managers were highly engaged, but with low talent in retail store management (their jobs), store performance actually dropped by an average of 5.9 percent below the baseline.

If store managers were not talented, but highly engaged, the stores actually did worse than the stores with low talent, disengaged managers.

Why is this?

When you dig in, it makes perfect sense. If store managers are highly engaged with low talent, they will be busy ... actively making more messes!

At least the low-talent, disengaged managers stay out of the way of store performance, due to their disengagement.

Clearly, we want talented, engaged employees. But the lesson here is to look for talent (read "skills to do the job") first, and then engagement second.

When it comes to hiring or growing managers, this means seeking specific management skills or tendencies, rather than focusing on the skills needed to generate results directly as an employee.

Perspective Shift: Hire specifically for management skills when hiring a manager.

For example, when it comes to sales and sales management, direct selling skills don't qualify a person to lead a team of salespeople as a sales manager. Whether in sales or any other department, it takes management skills to excel as a manager.

The Challenge of Choosing the Right Management Candidate

The fact is that the skills it takes to generate a result as an employee are different from the skills it takes to get results through others (the role of a manager).

In fact, further studies by the Gallup Organization have indicated that only one in ten people possess the talent to be a great manager.[7]

Of course, this also raises concerns about promoting people from within to management roles. When managers talk about developing the leadership skills of our newer employees, quite often we are talking about looking for those who are displaying management potential.

Unfortunately, many fall into the trap of taking the best person in the department and promoting that person to management. Usually, this results in less-than-ideal performance.

In dialogue with my team of consultants within our company, Kaizen Consulting, we identified two sets of skills that employees need to have before being considered for a management position. The first level or baseline of criteria consists of the attributes an employee needs to possess to be considered an A-Player in their own right. Yet not all A-Players would make great managers. The second level of criteria focuses directly on management potential, once A-Player status is established.

The Six Baseline Criteria for A-Player Employees

While not an exhaustive list, these are the minimum criteria an employee must have to be considered an A-Player over and above what is usually found in the core-value attributes for

---

[7]Ibid.

companies. We would not consider anyone for management who was not an A-Player in his/her own right. Other companies may have more criteria—for example, works well in a team environment is important in some companies, but not in others. These six criteria are just the bare minimum, and seem to apply to all companies.

1. Positive – Positivity psychologist Shawn Achor, in his May, 2011 TED Talk, *The Happy Secret to Better Work*, quoted statistics on the link between positivity and productivity.[8] According to Achor, people are 31 percent more productive when positive than when they are negative, neutral, or stressed. Salespeople are 37 percent more effective when positive, and medical doctors are 19 percent more accurate when positive, over those who are negative, neutral, or stressed.

So what is it about positivity that impacts effectiveness so much? I mean, I understand positive over negative, or even stressed, but positive over neutral? What gives?

It is not some esoteric thing. In fact, this is quite practical. When we are positive, the chemical dopamine is running through our systems. This is the body's natural "feel good" drug. Combined with serotonin, dopamine opens the neural pathways in the brain and quite literally improves our effectiveness.

Hence the presence of being positive as the first of the six baseline criteria to be an A-Player. If it has that much impact on effectiveness, we clearly need to include it.

2. Resourceful – We all know that people who look for innovative ways to solve problems are far more valuable to us than someone who constantly gets stuck, or gives up

---

[8]Available online at: www.ted.com/speakers/shawn_achor

when confronted with challenges. There are no shortages of challenges in any business.

Resourcefulness is considered by many to be the single most important attribute for any job applicant and for any type of role within a company. Personally, I agree. Without resourcefulness, we don't have an A-Player.

3. A bias for action – Most of us have heard about the three types of people:
- people who make things happen
- people who watch things happen
- people who wonder, "What happened?"

The people in the first category are the people who have a bias for action.

4. Strong at completion – Getting started is great. Yet, profit lies in completion. There is nothing more frustrating than to have to send someone back to finish a job, again and again. Or worse yet, to have to send others to go finish what the person started. If someone is not strong at getting things done and done well, then this person is not an A-Player for the role under consideration.

5. Anticipates well – This person is the most sought-after type of employee that exists. The ability to anticipate what is needed and then to provide it, either as it is required or just beforehand, is a skill that increases the value of someone immensely—truly the stuff of A-Players.

6. Looks to contribute – There are fundamentally two types of people: givers and takers. Givers give; takers take. A-Players give. There are those who are exceptionally skilled, but who become mercenaries. It is all about what they get for their superior skill. Who cares about the rest of the team? These people are not A-Players. It is as simple as that.

While these criteria tell us whether we are dealing with an A-Player, a definite requirement if we want to consider someone for management, they do not tell us whether or not that A-Player has management potential. What are the criteria to determine management potential? We have identified ten criteria.

THE TEN KEY CRITERIA TO DETERMINE MANAGEMENT POTENTIAL

Now that we have identified our A-Players, the next step is to determine their management potential. Remember, it is perfectly fine to have A-Players on our team who are fantastic doers, who—even with training—would not make good managers.

What skills and attributes do people have that differentiate the doers from the potentially great managers?

In order to answer this, we must first define the role of a manager, so that we know what we are seeking.

A manager's role is to transform the individual skills and talents of her group of employees into a coordinated and productive result for the department, project, or group that that manager oversees within the company. A *good* manager inspires her people. A *great* manager not only inspires her people, but also helps orchestrate the various talents of the people on her team to turn these individual efforts into one collective performance-based result.

There are a number of skills needed to do this. For experienced managers, we would be able to check on these factors, based on a candidate's track record of success in previous management roles.

However, for a budding potential manager, there is no track record of management to refer to, as none yet exists.

In order to determine if an employee has what it takes to be an effective manager, we need to assess their skills based on the following ten criteria.

1. Good listening skills - A manager needs to know what is going on with her employees. She needs to assess where people's real talents lie so she can orchestrate the coordinated performance of her department, and she needs to understand the underlying issues behind problems that arise in the normal course of operating a department, group, or project. This takes a strong level of awareness of people and the environment in which they work: a skill that is developed over time.

The precursor to this skill that we need to look for in a candidate is listening skills. In addition to being the prerequisite to awareness of others (we can't know what is going on with others if we don't listen), strong listening skills are essential to be able to read the environment—to identify issues and opportunities with staff, and between people, both within the department and outside it.

Without good listening skills, a candidate will not make an effective manager.

2. Big picture view - In order to orchestrate the performance of a diverse group of employees, a manager needs to understand and embrace the "bigger picture"—on two levels. First, the manager needs to be able to see how the various talents of his or her employees synthesize and add up to generating the overall objectives of that manager's department. Second, the manager needs to be able to see how his or her department's performance integrates with that of other departments to achieve the overall company objectives.

If a manager cannot see the big picture, this level of synthesis and prioritizing is not possible. Without this skill, everything seems like a big priority. Managers without this expanded perspective most often fail.

3. Calm/handles stress well - Part of the effectiveness of a manager lies in the ability to keep people focused on the job at hand. If a manager can't stay calm and handle stress, this lack of control invariably spills onto the rest of the team, generating negative impact. Handling stress well is critical to great management.

4. Patient - Let's face it. Employees won't always get it right. Patient managers develop their people. Impatient managers start jumping in and telling people what to do. Control freaks and micro-managers are the two most common demonstrations of a lack of patience within managers.

5. Strong discernment - A manager needs to be able to discern when an employee has a real difficulty, or when he is either fooling the boss, or fooling himself. She also needs to be able to see whether the company standards are being met, and where each project and initiative is relative to the goals and standards that have been set.

This takes strong discernment. If people have good judgment in their current role, they will likely be able to develop strong discernment in a management position. If people don't show strong, well-balanced judgment in their current role, management is probably not an option for them; at least not at this time.

6. Allows for people's humanity - We are all human. We make mistakes. A great manager allows for that. This is different from giving people the benefit of the doubt. If I give you the benefit of the doubt, when deep in my gut I know I shouldn't, then I do not trust my own intuition, which erodes my discernment.

On the other hand, if I know that you don't deserve the benefit of the doubt on something, I can call it what it really is (let's say it was an error in judgment that you made), yet still allow for your humanity (people make mistakes) and move on. Allowing for people's humanity is closely related to patience. Both are needed for effective management.

7. Good at articulating clearly - People who cannot articulate clearly have such a large impediment to effectiveness in working with others that the resulting misunderstandings will cost the company lots of time and money. This person is not a good management candidate.

8. Has the courage to say what needs to be said - Sometimes managers need to have difficult conversations with their people. If a slacker within a department is allowed to coast, this damages the morale of the whole department. If an individual has the courage to confront difficult situations in his current role, he is more likely to be relied upon to do so as a manager. This needs to be combined with strong discernment, but it remains an essential quality for effectiveness in management.

9. Actively seeks to learn - Notwithstanding this list of criteria, there are many more aspects to effectiveness in management. If someone is not hungry to learn, then that person won't grow as quickly. Great managers are always seeking to learn more, in the ever-changing environment of business.

10. Eager to ensure the success of others - To be an A-Player, someone needs to be a natural giver, someone who looks to contribute. To meet the standard of great management, more is needed. If someone is eager to ensure the success of others, then that will translate into the patience, discernment, and allowance for people's humanity: attributes that are all needed to be effective as a manager.

Louise's Reflections on Determining A-Players and Potential Managers

Louise commented on how she has been using the six criteria for an A-Player and the ten criteria for management potential.

"I have found these lists to be extremely useful," she said. "When interviewing potential employees, we can very quickly tell whether we have a strong candidate or not. We still go through all the different steps of recruitment and selection. Each different element of our process uncovers more pieces of the puzzle. By the time we are done, we can pretty much tell if the person will succeed with us.

"Also, when looking at our current people to determine who might have potential to become a manager, it is far easier to tell who has potential and who doesn't. For people who we don't see as future potential managers, we look for other pathways of growth in support of their career development, often as specialists in their respective roles.

"That way everyone wins," she said triumphantly.

"However," she continued. "There is one more misconception that I stumbled over as we have been growing and adding people. It has to do with titles."

TITLES MATTER: SELECTING JOB TITLES FOR EMPLOYEES

> **Misconception: Titles are an inexpensive way to make your people happy.**

To many people, job titles are very important. They represent one's status in a company to the outside world and among one's peers. If a company is static in size, this may not have a large impact. However, as a company grows, titles matter. Giving people titles for roles they are not performing can have large and very expensive negative consequences.

"I made the mistake of calling my first outside salesperson, Brad [not his real name], a sales manager," said Louise. "He told me that this title would make it easier for him to carry more credibility and to open more doors. Even though I hadn't specifically hired him as a sales manager, I said fine. I thought that if it would help him sell more, then so much the better.

"Then, when I added an account representative to that department, Brad started insisting that he should be her boss, since he had the title of Sales Manager. That became a problem."

I asked Louise, "You mentioned that you didn't specifically hire Brad as a sales manager. Did you consider him at all for management when you hired him?"

"I was thinking about it as a possibility at the time," she said. "However, it was more because I thought that if someone was good in sales, they could manage others. That was before I realized the different skills that managers need to properly support the people they manage.

"I didn't test him for management. I brought him in specifically for sales. After working with him for a bit, I found that he struggled to make sales, so there was no way I was going to make him the manager of that department. I knew he wouldn't fit as a manager, even before I saw the ten criteria."

"What happened?" I asked.

"I had to go through the process of taking his manager title away," she replied. "Later I had to let him go for lack of performance in sales. However, I did learn my lesson.

"Even if he really wanted the management role, I don't think I could have developed him in that way. Too much was missing. Now, with the lists of six A-Player criteria and ten management criteria, I see clearly a number of elements that just weren't there."

> **Perspective Shift: Be cautious about the titles you give people; these will likely change as you grow.**

It is always a safe plan to ensure that a title for someone accurately reflects their current role. If a title can be misconstrued to imply more, be cautious. Whether it is a salesperson who wants to be called a sales manager or a project coordinator who would prefer the title of project manager, it is better to address and clarify this up front.

The source of the title, at least as it pertains to managers, is relatively easy to address. If a person will be responsible for the results of others and those others report directly to that person, then the manager title may be applicable. If the person needs to facilitate with others without direct reporting lines, then either coordinator—for more junior roles—or even director for the senior roles (like marketing director) are often more appropriate than using the term manager. In this instance, the term director denotes a specialist rather than a manager of people. This is not to be confused with the title of director when it is applied to the board of directors who oversee the operation of a company. There are a number of companies that use the term Director to give people status as a professional or senior person within a company, without calling them managers. Under the right circumstances, this may work quite well.

Regardless of the initial title we give people, we may develop our people into larger roles over time, but to give a title that reaches beyond the scope of the role often has negative consequences, including potentially losing the person prematurely.

"Speaking of development, that is the next area for our review," I said.

"Great!" Louise exclaimed. "I am really looking forward to this part of our review. There has been so much good work done in the way people have grown."

Summary of Myths and Misconceptions

1. Myth: As a manager, never hire someone who is better than you. They could take your job.
2. Myth: The people who are best at their job make the best managers.
3. Misconception: Titles are an inexpensive way to make your people happy.

Summary of Perspective Shifts

1. If you cannot be replaced, you cannot be promoted.
2. Hire specifically for management skills when hiring a manager.
3. Be cautious about the titles you give people; these will likely change as you grow.

Six Baseline Criteria for Hiring A-Players

1. Positive
2. Resourceful
3. A bias for action
4. Strong at completion
5. Anticipates well
6. Looks to contribute

Ten Key Criteria to Determine Management Potential

1. Good listening skills
2. Big picture view
3. Calm/handles stress well
4. Patient
5. Strong discernment
6. Allows for people's humanity
7. Good at articulating clearly
8. Has the courage to say what needs to be said
9. Actively seeks to learn
10. Eager to ensure the success of others

10 DEVELOPING PEOPLE

"The growth and development of people is the highest calling of leadership."
Harvey S. Firestone, Founder of Firestone Tire and Rubber Company

In a fast-growing company, one of the most important elements of success is the growth and development of the people. There is very little that has as high a return on investment as people development. Sponge UK is no different in this respect. The development of Louise and her people was a major priority throughout our three years working together. This continues, as she progressively grows to higher levels.

"Well, Michael," Louise started, "the whole area of developing our people was one of those areas where I learned the most. To be honest, I really didn't think people you took on could change that much."

"Why was that?" I asked.

"I assumed that 'what you see is what you get.' But I was wrong. Our people have grown so much as the business has grown and it has come from places that I didn't really expect."

DEVELOPING STRONG LEADERS WITHIN A COMPANY

> **Misconception: People can't really grow all that much.**

"Why are you calling that a misconception instead of a myth?" she asked.

"Well, because it's true," I said, "but only in the short term. I have read a number of different studies and reports on the subject, and while people differ somewhat, on average, most neuroscientists agree that people can only grow between 5 percent and 15 percent ... at any single point in time. That's not very much. However, over a longer period of time, they can grow substantially."

> **Perspective Shift: People can grow between 5 percent and 15 percent ... at any single point in time. Over a longer period of time, they can grow substantially.**

Louise has seen many of her people grow quite substantially. She identified key staff in the four departments who could lead their teams, and she created a middle management group. Louise knew this was a key step if they were going to grow. The leadership responsibility needed to lie within the teams rather than with Kate, Matt, and Louise as directors. She didn't know if it would work, though.

"The challenge," said Louise, "was that they had no formal management training and although they were good at their job roles, managing others and getting the most from their teams was a whole other ball game."

"The leadership training we did with the managers, and all the core staff really made a difference," I commented.

"And it is still making a difference," she said. "To be truthful, I thought that leadership development was a 'nice-to-have', not essential for the company's growth."

> **Myth: Leadership development is not essential for the company's growth.**

"Do you still feel that way?" I asked, baiting her just a bit.

Louise laughed at this.

"You know I don't. That programme has made such a huge difference to both our managers and to our core staff that I'm convinced we wouldn't have achieved our current results without it," she said.

"That's pretty clear," I said, smiling.

"Yes, I thought you would like that," she said and chuckled.

> **Perspective Shift: Leadership Development is core to people's ability to grow.**

The most lucrative investment that a growing company can make is an investment in the development of its people. Louise had her doubts. She had to experience it herself to know that it is true. Looking at what she and her team have achieved, she is now a convert.

"The training for the managers has given them confidence in managing others," said Louise. "That has led to our departments flourishing, even as we struggle to find more staff.

"It also increased their awareness that managing people is a whole role in itself and not something you fit in around

147

whatever else you are doing. I had to learn that lesson too.

"As I was growing the sales team, more and more often, I was being 'interrupted' by these new salespeople to assist them with their proposals and questions, when I was trying to do my own sales. I realized that if we were going to achieve the sales we needed, I had to turn my thinking around. My focus needed to be around supporting them to achieve their sales, and turn them into confident salespeople. Although I would still need to deal with my own clients, supporting others and achieving excellent results through them became my priority.

"Now, there is a real feeling with the middle managers of growing the business together. I observe them helping each other with their issues or problems many times, instead of coming to me. This goes beyond what I expected.

"The complexities of moving from a small business of £400 thousand to over £2 million are huge. The challenge of balancing finances with people, processes, and sales is complicated enough. But add to this the growth and development of leaders and managers, so we could rise to these challenges, made for a cauldron of chaos.

"So, we have learned to work in a state of controlled chaos, making sure that the pot doesn't boil over. This means continuously reprioritizing, changing things quickly when they aren't working or doing more of what is working."

"Doesn't that scare you at all?" I asked.

"Not at all," said Louise.

"It means that coming into work every day is exciting. I have never had so much fun in my life!

"If I ever question what we are doing, I just have to look at the growth of our managers. I look at what each of them has done, and how they have grown."

We often talk about growing people. But what does that look like in reality? Louise provided three examples of how the company's managers have grown and evolved as the business has grown.

Alan – Development Manager

"Alan originally came to us as a university placement student," said Louise, "during his third year at university. He proved himself as very capable. After a year, he went back to university, got a degree, and we offered him a job so he returned to us.

"By 2010, Alan demonstrated that he could carry out development tasks to time, on budget, and to high quality. We knew we could trust him to do his job well. At that point, we took on three more developers. Jamie, Fin, and Will initially assisted Alan as colleagues.

"In 2011-12, Alan became responsible for the development team, working in conjunction with Alex, who was promoted to lead the studio team. When he started, he was doing his debriefs weekly with me in the same meeting along with Alex.

"Then Alan started creating checklists to ensure consistent quality. The other developers were given responsibility for their own work. Alan then created standard costing templates to provide more accurate costing for module production. This helped everyone out, and allowed us to be more effective in our job costing and project resource allocations.

"Eventually, Alan started to do debriefs with me without Alex.

"Then, in 2013, when a large project came in that required hiring multiple developers, Alan planned how the work would be done, hired the developers we needed, and trained them so they were up to speed quickly to work to his standards.

"Alan also provided (and still provides) technical solutions for other managers and the directors. He has been attending meetings and liaising with clients, troubleshooting and solving their problems. He also oversees all computers and IT in the office.

"In addition to his role heading up the developers, Alan has provided costs for tenders and bids. He established the creation of templates as the way of controlling costs and efficient working.

"He undertook the leadership training for middle managers and created roles and responsibilities for developers, defining the different levels of that role. He is part of the management team and helps define policies and clarify processes.

"When the role of second-in-command was advertised within Alan's team, Jon applied for and was given the job. Alan has been training Jon in the developer leadership role.

"Alan has also been gaining knowledge and understanding of the entire production process from instructional designer, to design, to development, and he carries out QAs to ensure quality production.

"In addition to his own team, Alan provides mentoring support to other staff outside his department. Together with Helen, our Office Manager, he orchestrated the office move of twenty-nine people seamlessly with minimal down time.

"Alan has been busily at work of late, on specific operational projects such as assisting with recruitment."

Alex – Design Studio Manager

"Alex originally worked for my design and marketing business, before Sponge began," Louise explained. "When we decided that we would only focus on elearning, he came to work for Sponge. He is very passionate about design and is an excellent all-rounder, good at typography, illustration, and design, and has a meticulous eye for detail. He gets elearning and knows how design can make it easier for the learner to grasp concepts using visual ideas.

"Alex cares deeply about what he does and he has suffered with stress occasionally. The quality of his work is never affected and he will always meet a deadline, but the stress has on occasion manifested itself in him becoming ill with headaches and colds and viruses. He does have small children so that probably increases the germ pool but even still, it is something that I need to be mindful of. He is so committed; he keeps soldiering on, even when feeling ill.

"Michael, on your first visit in 2011, you suggested a management structure that would place Alex as head of the studio with Alan assisting him. Alex helped Alan grow in confidence as, initially, Alan didn't always want to speak up or raise any issues with me. This worked well for a while until both design and development teams grew and they both became heads of their departments in their own right.

"I think becoming a manager of a team of designers has been a challenge for Alex, as he is such a hands-on designer. He was so busy with his own work, he didn't have time to oversee or check other designers' work.

"However, he has really risen to that challenge. Alex now has five in his team and is recruiting another five. In order to manage more effectively, he makes sure that he leaves some of his time free each day so he can help others. I have observed him assisting others and can see what an impact this has, both on him and on them. A simple comment or piece of design direction advice can save a designer hours of work, which makes Alex feel good.

"Alex is very excited about setting up and running Sponge University, which has been scheduled for launch with the design team in February of 2015. This endeavor helps him fulfill his desire for continuous improvement and excellent design in elearning. He is working closely with Louise H. and Glen, two other designers on his team. Together they have assembled a year's syllabus of training courses each month for the design team. It includes sessions that draw on expertise within other departments as well as external experts to help the design team deepen their knowledge on effective elearning design.

"Alex is a valued member of the management team," Louise concluded, "working closely with the other managers to help make Sponge a great place to work and to create elearning we can be proud of. His passion for design has helped establish Sponge as a distinct company in the elearning marketplace."

Kate – The Challenger Daughter

"Kate has worked with me for most of the time since we started Sponge," said Louise. "She has had a couple of spells working in New York, but for the most part has been by my side helping me grow the business. Now when I say by my side, I need to qualify this.

"Probably prodding my side would be a more accurate description. It is in her nature to challenge everything. She'd think about how our elearning could be more creative, what other services we could provide our clients, how we could measure effectiveness consistently, how our processes could be improved, and how we could introduce more quality standards and more consistent internal training plans for staff.

"She worked with the production team to clarify and document our processes for improved efficiency. When we decided to build a new LMS (Learning Management System), she took on this twelve-month project, defining all features from the customer's perspective and working closely overseeing the development team. She was also instrumental in the decision to hire Chris, who manages the LMS development team.

"For someone who likes to create processes, she can also disrupt them in the name of creativity and keeping the client happy. She's been known to intervene with the instructional design team, graphic design team, or the development team if she thinks it could be more creative or effective. And sometimes in the early days, this hadn't made her popular all the time. She has learned over the years how to give constructive criticism in softer ways. People couldn't argue with her suggestions, as they consistently would leave the clients better off.

"Kate loves to push the boundaries," Louise continued. "She has been behind every award we have won. She is a robust creative thinker. Unlike some I've worked with who give you half-baked ideas, Kate comes up with productive and innovative ideas and is able to think something through from initial concept right to the end.

"Our product mix would not be anywhere as strong as it is if it weren't for her. With the help of her fellow managers, she has led us to real depth and award-winning results.

"As her mother and boss, it hasn't always been easy. We once tried to share an office together. To put it simply, this was a disaster. Two strong-minded women in a small space doesn't work. Kate is rebellious, always wanting things to be better. This challenger spirit combined with her loyalty and commitment has underpinned our growth and success along the way.

"Her commitment to her own learning and to the growth of our company is also clear. While working full-time with us, she decided to do an MBA. I'm not sure how she did it, but she pulled it off, gaining a distinction for her dissertation, and growing immeasurably in the process."

Emerging Leaders Programme

Sponge participated in a yearlong, multifaceted leadership development programme offered through my company. This programme, with three distinct levels, trains groups of people as follows:

1. Emerging Leaders - How to generate results at a whole new level
2. Middle Leaders - How to achieve superior performance, through others
3. Top Leaders - How to create and unfold a compelling future

"Michael, the Emerging Leaders Programme that we conducted for our core team has made a big difference as well," Louise said. "Like so much of what we have talked about, I was surprised by just how much of an impact this initiative had.

"A few months into this programme, I recall walking through the office and noticing a palpable energy in the air. Developers were discussing an elearning module they were working on with the project managers.

"In the meantime, I saw designers huddled together reviewing some visuals on a screen, and instructional designers in a briefing. There was a positive buzz in the atmosphere that we didn't have before to such an extent. This buzz was in large part due to the Emerging Leaders Programme where people were trained to think of themselves as 'go-to' people and that their contribution really mattered to the business.

"This brings up another misconception I had. I always figured that with people busy with their jobs, doing, it would be up to the management team to identify, set up, and implement major improvements and new initiatives for the company's growth."

Implementing Major Improvements Within the Company

> **Misconception: It is solely management's responsibility to set up and implement major improvements and initiatives for the company's growth.**

Louise added, "What I discovered was that people are happy to take on substantial projects, if given the chance."

> **Perspective Shift: People will take on substantial projects, if given the chance.**

The leadership training gave people a reason to step into some project work, which enhanced the company in many significant ways.

"What are some of the projects they have taken on?" I asked.

Rebranding Project

"As part of the programme," said Louise, "each person had to take on a project of their choice. One of the projects that has had the biggest impact on the business was our Sponge rebrand. Our branding had been the same for ten years and we thought it was about time it changed. It did look very dated.

"Glen decided to take on this project. This was going to be challenging for him, as both Kate and I had a strong design background and would want to input our own ideas. Glen involved the whole team in the process, interviewing them, and reviewing client feedback on what they liked about Sponge.

Based on this, Glen moved forward with this project. The results were amazing. We generated five times the amount of business from the Learning Technologies Exhibition, won best stand at the CIPD conference, and web enquiries doubled."

Improving Translation Services Project

Louise continued, "Dan took on improving our translation services to better meet our clients' needs. We were already doing this but he went deeper, exploring better processes and systems we could use to make our service more efficient and quicker for global rollouts. He managed to reduce a typical translation project from twelve weeks to four weeks, which was amazing. Once the better processes were established, he trained our solutions advisors so they could more easily explain the services to clients."

Other Key Projects

"As well as individual projects, there were cross-functional group projects. One of these is an online induction programme for new starters with our company. In addition, the sales, marketing, and design teams are working on a sales toolkit to assist the solutions advisors," Louise concluded.

Sponge University

As an organization, not only is Sponge UK committed to helping their clients' staff learn and grow, but is it also a key purpose of their core organization. A really exciting development they are piloting is the creation of an ongoing learning and development initiative they are calling Sponge University.

Louise explained. "Sponge University is a system of learning that we are developing, comprised of a series of yearlong programmes within each of the different departments. The staff of that department may gain access to continued education and learning, in collaboration with each other. In each case, there is a curriculum, assigned instructors, and an overall theme for the year, for each month, and for each session (two per month).

"We are trialing this with the design team who have already developed their twelve-month curriculum. Every month for two half-day sessions, they have a guest speaker, and a practical hands-on activity to put into practice what they have learned. Once the difficulties are smoothed out and the programme is confirmed as successful, this will be rolled out by the Instructional Design and Development teams, as well as by Project Management."

"Were there any training and development failures?" I asked Louise.

"Yes, there was one in particular a few years back," she said. "This led to one of the most important lessons I learned. While you can grow people, I thought that you could grow someone into who you need them to be. Then they can do the job you wanted them to do in the first place."

"Ouch!" I winced, knowing the trap she had entered.

PROFESSIONAL DEVELOPMENT

> **Myth: You can "grow" (read "change") people into who you want/need them to be, so then they can do the job you wanted done in the first place.**

"So, if I can be so bold as to read between the lines," I conjectured, "you hired someone who was really nice, hoping they would fit the role you needed. Then when they didn't fit, instead of letting them go, you kept trying to train them into being what you were already paying for. Would that pretty much summarize it?"

"Yes, that was it; spot on!" she said. "You have seen this one before, haven't you?"

> **Perspective Shift: Make sure you are getting value from people at their current job. Then you can grow them.**

"Yes, I have seen this, many times," I replied, "even in our own company back when it started. This is why our hiring processes that you are also using are so robust. We have all failed here initially. This is a very common trap for entrepreneurs—especially the ones with big hearts—to fall into. You really want the person to fit into the job, even if he doesn't actually fit. Then you try to 'train' him into it. The goal is to hire people who can already do a job well, and let them do that, rather than hoping they will grow into it."

"That's just expensive," I said, and she agreed.

"Lesson learned, the hard way," she said. "Now we make sure the person wants to and is capable of doing the job that they are applying for, rather than hope they will fit because they are nice, or we are too busy to look further. Also, if someone isn't working out in their role, we are getting better at telling the truth earlier, rather than just hoping they will grow into the role. I know that hope is not a strategy," she chuckled and said.

"There were two other misconceptions I had, both around performance reviews."

> **Misconception: Employees treat reviews as a chance to get more money. Keep salary reviews connected with professional development reviews.**

If salary reviews are done at the same time as the professional development review, people will tune out the professional development, and wait patiently to see what, if any raise will be forthcoming. When this is done, the opportunity for staff to grow is diminished dramatically.

> **Perspective Shift: Separate salary reviews from professional development reviews.**

By separating professional development from salaries, people will treat their development far more seriously. The difference in their growth is clearly demonstrable.

Louise commented, "Once we separated these two types of reviews, we found that people expressed far more interest in their own growth. They were having more fun, too."

The other misconception had to do with timing of reviews.

> **Misconception: To minimize the interruption of professional development reviews, do them all together, at the same time each year.**

Managers often complain that reviews take too much of their time away from other priorities. This thinking sows the seeds of dissatisfaction and results in the deterioration of staff morale. Business owners don't realize just how much their employees count on reviews to gain feedback on their work. This is especially true in a company that professes a commitment to the growth and development of its people.

Staff who are concerned about their growth within a company generally put a real effort into preparing for these reviews.

As a company grows, it becomes more and more difficult for managers to take the time to do these really effectively and in-depth, especially if they are all done at once.

One common complaint by employees regarding reviews is that they are the ones to come up with all the ideas. Their bosses ask great questions, but don't give useful feedback. This is usually the work of a very effective manager, who hasn't taken the time to prepare. This is frustrating to employees—especially great ones—who are seeking feedback and ways to improve. Too often they leave the review feeling underwhelmed. Because they are the great employees, we don't usually hear the feedback. Yet it has an impact in any event. This could land as subtle discouragement, or feeling surprised and less appreciated than they thought they were. Not the message we intend to send to our people.

> **Perspective Shift: Move professional development reviews to the employee's work anniversary with the company.**

With the levels of growth that have been occurring at Sponge, it is getting harder for the managers to deal with the time it takes to do proper professional development reviews. As a result, Louise is trying a new initiative. She has some of her department heads experimenting with holding staff development reviews on the anniversary of when an employee joined the company.

Salary reviews, which are separate, are still done at the same time of the year. However, by setting up the professional development reviews in line with when people joined the company, the managers have spread out the reviews to be done in smaller pieces, throughout the year.

Louise said, "I was surprised just how hungry our people are to gain their supervisor's perspective on their growth achieved, and where they could improve. People want to get better. We need to give them that chance.

"We are committed to the growth of our people. A couple of our managers complained a bit at first that moving reviews to people's work anniversaries meant that such reviews never go away. After thinking about it, they realized that we don't want the conversation of people's growth to ever go away. We are slowly working our way through the staff, to make this change. That way we can demonstrate to people how much of a priority we place on their learning and growth."

A Tool to Help With Professional Development

One of the things that managers discover is that doing reviews can be tough, both on the manager, who consistently has multiple priorities and projects on the go, and also to staff, who are responding to the needs of their bosses.

A tool that a couple of Louise's managers are testing is a simple tracking tool that catches both the measurable deliverables for the different projects within the department, and also the learning that is occurring by each staff member.

The thinking behind this is that in a learning organization, people want to be achieving both project results and learning on every single project.

Entitled **Project Deliverables and Intended Learning**, this tracking sheet is broken into three distinct parts. Part 1 has space for the employee to list the deliverables that are required for successful completion of the project. This is not a task list, but the actual end-result (the deliverable) to be achieved. To the right, for each deliverable is a column for the due date and another column for the date the deliverable is achieved.

Part 2 is a space for the employee to list what she/he intends to learn from this project, again with due dates. Part 3 holds a space for after the project is concluded, where the employee can list any other learning or discoveries that occurred during the project.

Collecting these sheets at the end of each project makes it easier for the manager to properly prepare for and hold powerful professional development reviews as well. Once again, everyone wins.

Louise commented on the introduction and testing of this simple tracking sheet.

"Before introducing these tracking sheets," said Louise, "we had been asking people what they have learned that day when the managers were doing stand-ups at the end of the day. People often just make up things.

"However, when learning is planned in advance, we find that the learning and growth are accelerated. People are more conscious and proactive about their own growth. I'm looking forward to seeing the impact of this new tracking sheet. It is still early days for this, but so far the acceptance is good, and the feedback is strong."

"Excellent!" I said.

"Let's move into reviewing your progress in sales and marketing," I suggested, to which Louise agreed.

Summary of Myths and Misconceptions

1. Misconception: People can't really grow all that much.
2. Myth: Leadership development is not essential for the company's growth.
3. Misconception: It is solely management's responsibility to set up and implement major improvements and initiatives for the company's growth.
4. Myth: You can "grow" (read "change") people into who you want/need them to be, so then they can do the job you wanted done in the first place.
5. Misconception: Employees treat reviews as a chance to get more money. Keep salary reviews connected with professional development reviews.
6. Misconception: To minimize the interruption of professional development reviews, do them all together, at the same time each year.

Summary of Perspective Shifts

1. People can grow between 5 percent and 15 percent ... at any single point in time. Over a longer period of time, they can grow substantially.
2. Leadership Development is core to people's ability to grow.
3. People will take on substantial projects, if given the chance.
4. Make sure you are getting value from people at their current job. Then you can grow them.
5. Separate salary reviews from professional development reviews.

6. Move professional development reviews to the employee's work anniversary with the company.

Tools Introduced in this Chapter

The Project Deliverables and Intended Learning Sheet

Section 3: Sales and Marketing

"Catch a man a fish, and you can sell it to him. Teach a man to fish, and you ruin a wonderful business opportunity."
Author Unknown[9]

---

[9]This quote is often attributed to Karl Marx. However, the true origin is not known.

11 EXPANDING OUR SALES PROCESS

"If people like you, they'll listen to you, but if they trust you, they'll do business with you."
Zig Ziglar

Increasing sales is essential for growth. Louise and Kate had been the two people bringing in all the sales for the company. Louise knew that this would need to shift if she were to achieve her goals for increased growth and profit. To do that, she would need to build a sales team. However, before building a sales team, we discussed the need to expand the company's sales process.

Louise has always had good success when it came to gaining new business. Yet things evolved for her and Kate in this area over the past three years.

Louise said, "I wasn't sure what to expect when we started addressing our sales. I remember when you suggested that Kate and I take your sales training course. I didn't really know what to expect, but thought we should give it a try.

"I had never had formal sales training, and I figured that

the skills and tools you talked about might help both Kate and me. Also, it would be something she and I would share in common. I really wanted Kate involved more in the growth of the company, and I felt that this would be a great way for the two of us to work on something together. Hopefully we would pick up some useful tips along the way."

"What were some of the things you learned that made the biggest difference to your sales?" I asked.

"For me," said Louise, "the whole approach you introduced seemed on the surface to be quite similar to what we had been doing all along. However, as we got beneath the surface, it wasn't the same at all. You encouraged us to look from a different perspective, which changed everything. There were a number of very subtle distinctions I learned that helped me reframe how we now approach the whole area of sales. Now, we talk with our clients very differently, in subtle ways, taking a more effective approach from how we engaged them before."

UNDERSTANDING YOUR BUSINESS FROM YOUR CLIENT'S POINT OF VIEW

> **Misconception: I have been running my business a long time. I obviously know how to talk about what we do.**

When Louise and Kate were given the first exercise in the programme, to build their company credo, Louise started to wonder out loud whether this would be a trivial exercise or a waste of time. Because she had been in business for years, she thought it would be obvious that she was in the best position to describe what Sponge did for others.

"I was very quickly surprised at just how hard it was when I looked at it through our client's eyes," she said.

"That's true," I said. "You do know your business from the inside out. Nobody else knows it as intimately as you do, from that vantage point.

"And that is the heart of the problem. There is a very common trap where business owners and core salespeople get stuck, without even knowing it. We see the business so clearly from our own perspective that we assume that the client's needs and our solutions are as obvious to them as they are to us. After all, why would the customer be here if they didn't need our goods or services?"

"That's exactly how I felt," Louise commented. "Our leads have been primarily based upon people contacting us. They all needed elearning solutions. However, what I discovered was that being **inside** the business could make it difficult to describe what we do from the perspective of people **outside** the business.

"For me, writing our credo was all about helping me see our business from the perspective of outsiders and how our services would impact them. Before this, we had been talking about the business from our point of view, not theirs."

The Credo

The credo is a simple tool that helps clarify the core of a business. What is the result that clients and customers seek to gain from working with us? Unlike an elevator pitch, which talks about what we do, the credo doesn't describe our product or service offering. Instead, it focuses on results for the customer. Our products and services are just the mechanisms to help get to that result. By addressing the credo, we are forced to look from our customers' perspectives, and the results they need.

The thing to remember is that customers who purchase

anything from anyone are buying access to one thing—change.

By understanding the specific result that our clients and customers seek, we may then determine whether we are in a position to assist them to achieve that particular result with our products and services.

The credo is formed by answering four simple questions. They are:

1. Who am I?
2. What is the result I assist customers to achieve?
3. Who are my customers?
4. What is the impact on them from achieving their desired result?

Notice that nowhere does it ask to state the product or service. Since the product or service offering is merely the mechanism to assist the client in achieving their desired result, it doesn't have a place in the credo. Our product is not the desired result itself.

While there are four different questions to address within the credo, if the second question is properly addressed, we are in much better shape to respond to the rest.

THE TWO CORE FUNDAMENTAL CONCEPTS OF BUSINESS

There are two core fundamental concepts of any business:

1. The Value Exchange
2. Relationships in Business

The Value Exchange

The first core fundamental concept of business is the "value exchange." Simply put, the value exchange refers to the exchange of our profit, the part that we get in a transaction, in return for providing our clients and customers with a product or a service that has either quantitative or qualitative value for them—the part they get.

If it is a better deal for our customers to give us their money than it is to keep it for themselves, or give it to our competitors, they will give that money to us. Similarly, if it is a better deal for us to take their money and provide them with our product or service, we will do that too.

That is the value exchange.

This may sound simple (and it is!), but it is also the entire core of every single business that exists on the planet. Without the value exchange, there is no business. The synergy that is generated from this exchange is how wealth is created in the world. An entrepreneur who is not good at the value exchange doesn't usually last in business for very long.

A Common Complaint: External Factors

Commonly, as people in business, we complain when we are having difficulties in sales. We blame our difficulties on a poor economy, shifts in world markets, or even cheaper competitors—often referred to as "bottom-feeders"—the ones who spoil the market for the good guys (that's us).

Yet these factors are often far less relevant than the lack of clarity of the value exchange.

When we don't get clear, positive responses from our clients and customers, it is usually not because of economic conditions, competitors, or other external factors. Those elements definitely impact a business. Yet, too often the lack of results is due to a lack of transparency of the value exchange.

How clear is it from our customer's perspective that they will gain value from us? From our view, it may be perfectly clear. What about from their view? To answer that, we need to place ourselves in their world. Hence, the specific questions in the credo.

RELATIONSHIPS IN BUSINESS

Relationships are the second core fundamental element of business. Much is talked about regarding the importance of relationships in business. Yet, most people don't really know what constitutes an effective business relationship. We all know it when we are in one, and we can describe the results of having these relationships. But, what is the basis of relationships in business?

There are four levels of relationships:

1. professional
2. personal
3. structural
4. power

To the surprise of many, the primary level of relationship in business is NOT personal. If the personal relationship were the first basis for doing business with someone, then we would be, by definition, willing to do business with everyone we know personally or socially.

That is certainly not the case for me (nor for most people I know). There are many people who I know personally and whose company I enjoy, but with whom I definitely would not want to do business. That doesn't mean they are bad people. I just need certain things when I transact business with people, and not all my friends have all those things. For example, I may need a well-developed level of competence in a particular area from a supplier. I could be a good friend of someone who is new in that business, but if he doesn't have the skill I need, I won't do business with him. At least I won't for that particular purpose.

All relationships are based in trust and confidence. A **professional relationship** (the primary level in business) occurs when our customer has trust and confidence in two things. First, when we give our word we will keep it. If they can't trust our word, they have no basis to believe that we will deliver what we say, nor that they will be better off by doing business with us. This is fundamental to business.

That's why it is important to keep even our small promises. Many people intuitively judge how we keep all our promises by how we deal with the small ones. That's why showing up on time makes a difference. If I can't get to where I say when I say it, how am I to be trusted on larger issues, like meeting client deadlines for major purchases?

The second element of a professional relationship occurs when the customer has trust and confidence that they will be better off as a result of buying our goods and services than if they bought from our competitor, or not at all.

The professional relationship is effectively about the value exchange. If our customers have confidence that they will be better off by working with us, they will. Their trust in this summarizes the value exchange.

While the **personal relationship** is not the primary reason to do business with someone, it definitely has an influence. Therefore, it is second. After all, we tend to do more business with people that we like rather than people that we don't like.

The third level of relationship is a **structural relationship**. Examples of this include someone's computer person, someone's accountant, someone's life insurance agent, or someone's business consultant. Often these relationships are based upon a deep personal trust of the service provider's capability and commitment.

This is a very individual relationship. That is, where I (instead of "we" in this case) personally become part of my customer's structure or method of doing business. I don't just get most of their business, and I don't just get to quote on bids every time there is a need. I become that part of the business, on an outsourced basis, for them.

In fact if my competitor approaches my client, either they

chuckle with me about it, or they send the competitor directly to me to determine whether our competitor's products are things I might consider and recommend.

The fourth level of relationship is called a **power relationship.** This is what emerges instead of a structural relationship if there are multiple people involved with a customer, and the customer can and does rely on any of the people to generate the desired result (not just me). This relationship is just as deep as the structural relationship. However, it is not with one individual (me), but includes others in the organization as well. There is usually such a strong consistency in levels of product or service delivery that the customer doesn't care whether it is me or someone else who serves them, as long as it is someone from our firm.

> **Perspective Shift: Take the client's perspective.**
> **Place ourselves in their world.**

This is something that many business owners and salespeople never get. They continue to speak to clients and customers about products and services, and advantages and benefits, and see life from their own perspective, rather than to truly put themselves into the client's shoes.

Louise weighed in on this.

"When Kate and I looked," she said, "we were speaking about our products and services from our perspective, not our clients'. That exercise changed how we now talk about our business. We are far more customer-friendly than we were before. We always cared about our customers, but we talked about us too much, and them not enough.

"Now that I have attuned my listening to this over the past few years, I really notice when people in sales talk about our needs as their customers, or whether they are focused on them and their products. Most people talk about themselves.

"Sometimes, I receive emails from suppliers wanting to work with us. These emails are all about how great they are, how long they have been established, who they work for, or their technical skills. I usually just delete these emails, as they have nothing to do with us. The emails I keep and follow up on are the ones where the supplier shows an interest in us, what is important to us, from our perspective, not just about their great products."

EXPANDING THE SELLING PROCESS

> **Misconception: Clients just want a proposal with pricing and deliverables. The sooner we give that to them, the sooner they will buy.**

There was another change in perspective that Louise gained when she and Kate did the sales training. That related to the use of a more organized and expanded selling process.

It made a really big difference to them. Before that, Louise thought that her job was really just to give clients their proposal with pricing and deliverables. That is what they requested, so she always thought, "The sooner we give that to them, the sooner they will buy."

> **Perspective Shift: Take the time to understand client needs in depth. It makes a big difference.**

As Louise participated in sales training, her perspectives on sales changed. She evolved her process of acquiring new clients to encompass an expanded process.

Expanded Selling Process

You always need a relationship sufficient to do business. There is an expanded relationship management process developed by Kaizen Consulting that Louise and her team have adopted.

In this extensive and detailed process of gaining more customers at a profit, the focus is on managing business relationships with customers. The two primary levels to manage are the professional and the personal levels of relationship—addressing the value exchange and the likeability factor.

The whole notion, as it applies to acquiring new customers, is to slow the selling process down and understand clients and customers in more depth, in order to speed up the result, regardless of what that result might be. With this process, we get farther faster, by slowing the process in the early stages.

Louise and her team adopted the new selling process with great success.

Louise's Perspective on the New Selling Process

"Michael," said Louise, "you first introduced Kate and me to an expanded version of a selling process in the sales training course you provided. Even though I had never really had any formal training, I had worked in sales for a long time. In fact, for over twenty years I had run my own businesses and had to be able to sell to survive. If I am honest, I thought I was pretty good at it. It was something that came instinctively to me. Despite that, I was curious to see what else I could learn on the course.

"You broke down the customer acquisition process into phases. You encouraged us to focus on building customer relationships—as you defined them—rather than selling. A key point was that we slow down the first part of the process—where we clarify and understand our clients' needs—before jumping into providing solutions. Too often, we would make our recommendations before really understanding what the client wanted, in depth.

Louise continued, "The first time I used the training was with a large global insurance company that had approached us for a proposal. Before the training, I would have probably had an initial chat to understand what they needed, and gone straight to a proposal.

"With the expanded process, I first spoke with them to see if they were right for us and we were right for them. I then used the list of fact-finding questions we had revised and developed on the course, so I could go much deeper on their requirements. Then, in a step before making recommendations, I fed my understanding of their situation back to them to check and make sure I got it right. I found that this step, when separated out from the proposal, had a significant impact. By clarifying with a client what we heard in advance of preparing the proposal, the trust level rose. We were demonstrating that we listened well and that we cared enough to check in and make sure we understood what was important to our client.

"After the potential client reviewed this and came back with a few comments, I then reconsidered the solution and did my proposal. Overall, this took about one to two weeks, but it was worth it in the end as we won the work, and it was for a much larger scope than I had originally imagined."

A Problem Solved

Before introducing this expanded process, one common problem Louise faced when new people first started was that they were mixing up client requirements with the solutions. For example, they would describe the client's technical requirements and then immediately describe how they could solve it. The problem with this method of jumping to solutions was that her staff weren't taking the time to really focus on the client's requirements, issues, and challenges. They made assumptions and went from there. As a result, some client needs were either missed or ineffectively addressed.

"Now," said Louise, "we delve more deeply into client requirements, seeking to understand the issues beneath the surface ones that clients tell us. As a result, there are more opportunities to create better and more effective solutions. Having these detailed discovery meetings to really ensure a core understanding of our clients' requirements is key. I also find that if potential clients aren't that interested in answering questions or having a discussion at this level, then it is unlikely they are that interested in doing business with us. They are just price shopping, regardless of value or the fit to their needs."

Michael's Observations on Louise's Perspective Shift

From this process, Louise incorporated three fundamental shifts. The first was to take the client's perspective—to look from their eyes, not her own— when opening the relationship. The company's materials and how Louise introduces herself to new customers reflect this change.

Based upon the increased trust from taking their perspective, Louise generated increased access to the second shift, which was to go far deeper in her fact-finding with clients, to really understand their underlying core needs, not just the surface ones they presented when they inquired about Sponge's services.

The third shift was to complete the feedback loop with clients, before ever presenting a proposal to them. By demonstrating that she understood the clients at depth, not only is she able to provide better solutions (from the better information), those solutions are being better received by clients as well.

After the training, the company embedded this expanded selling process into their standard operating processes. Now when new learning solutions advisors start, they get training in this methodology, as a core part of the company's methodology. The results are definitely worth the extra effort.

Misconception: Since I already know how to sell, this is not an area that I need to focus on. Other priorities need my attention.

Michael, while I thought I knew sales quite well, and I did to a certain level, I didn't think that this area needed more of my focus and attention," Louise admitted. "Had you not suggested that I participate, I'm sure I would not have done this training from you or anyone else. I really thought it was handled. There are so many other priorities in growing that needed my attention that I thought I should focus on those."

I asked, "What do you believe now?"

She pondered for a moment before speaking.

"Well, in business, there are always going to be competing priorities, but when you get down to it, our clients are at the core of why we are here. We are an organization about learning and development supporting our clients, as well as our own learning. As a company, we need to continually learn how to support them better. This includes improving our listening skills with them, even before they choose to work with us."

Perspective Shift: We owe it to our clients to continually improve. That includes improving our listening skills with them, even before they choose to do business with us.

It takes a real commitment to learning, growth, and constant improvement to invest in our own listening skills, especially with people before they even buy from us. Yet, this is exactly how Louise felt, and explains in part why she and her team are as successful as they are.

"That sounds like a pretty powerful statement," I said. "Not everyone in business believes that, or is that passionate about it."

She responded. "Others can believe what they want. I can only speak for us. If we are not willing to really understand, at depth, what our clients need from us, and support them in all their decisions around our work together, including whether or not to work with us, then what are we doing here? The core of who we are doesn't get much deeper than this commitment to their care, and continually learning how to do it better.

"Having had the privilege of working closely with your managers and other budding leaders," I commented, "I know that this commitment runs through your entire organization. I think that is one of the reasons that your company delivers such strong work and solid results."

"Don't get me wrong," Louise responded, "we definitely have our bumps and hiccups, the problems and frustrations of periodically falling short on our commitments, but it is not for any lack of heart, or giving it our best. I am very fortunate to work with the people we have on our team."

"I think you are all fortunate to work with each other," I added. "Are there any other shifts in perspectives that you gained in the area of sales?"

"Yes, there is one," she commented. "I always thought that competitors, especially larger competitors with deeper pockets—who were anyone other than us at the time—were to be feared, mistrusted, and actively avoided."

> **Myth: Competitors—especially bigger ones—are to be feared, mistrusted, and actively avoided.**

"When we were smaller," said Louise, "our clients always asked us about our competitors and how we were different. I didn't always have good responses, other than that we cared more and that we were more innovative and creative. I couldn't prove it though, so I always felt like I was on the defensive.

"Even the banks, when asking for our business plan for lines of credit and loans, would ask us about our competitors. I really thought they were a big deal."

> **Perspective Shift: Competitors will get their share of business and so will we. We need to focus on what we do and on our clients.**

"It sounds like you think differently now," I observed.

"Definitely!" she asserted. "Now, I don't pay much attention to them at all. I think very differently about competitors. We will get our business, and they will get theirs. The business that may be good for them is not always what is good for us, and vice versa. I know it is not always like that, but they are definitely not to be feared. They are people supporting their clients, just like us. They have different strengths and attract different clients.

"In fact, we are doing some joint venture projects with a couple of our competitors now. There are a lot of really talented people we are working with. In one of the projects we are doing, where we are developing new technological improvements that will help us all, our developers on that project are doing well and having a great time, in collaboration with others from other companies."

"That's great! Any other shifts in this area?" I asked.

"Not unless you count the entire development of a sales department," Louise replied, smiling.

"Ok," I said. "Let's go there next."

Summary of Myths and Misconceptions

1. Misconception: I have been running my business a long time. I obviously know how to talk about what we do.
2. Misconception: Clients just want a proposal with pricing and deliverables. The sooner we give that to them, the sooner they will buy.
3. Misconception: Since I already know how to sell, this is not an area I need to focus on. Other priorities need my attention.
4. Myth: Competitors—especially bigger ones—are to be feared, mistrusted, and actively avoided.

Summary of Perspective Shifts

1. Take the client's perspective. Place ourselves in their world.
2. Take the time to understand client needs in depth. It makes a big difference.
3. We owe it to our clients to continually improve. That includes improving our listening skills with them, even before they choose to do business with us.
4. Competitors will get their share of business and so will we. We need to focus on what we do and on our clients.

Summary of Tools

1. The Credo
   a. Who am I?
   b. What is the result I assist customers to achieve?
   c. Who are my customers?

    d. What is the impact on them from achieving their desired result?

2. An Expanded Selling Process

    a. Follow the three Key and Constant Elements:

        i. Take your customer's perspective

        ii. Clarify their gain

        iii. Build trust and confidence

    b. Build and then ask questions two levels deeper than your best competitor would. Get to the core, the underlying issues.

    c. Complete the feedback loop by restating, either orally or in writing, what you heard from your customer. Send this to them right after your fact-finding meeting as a separate item, not just at the start of a proposal.

    d. Ensure that your solutions are tied directly to the stated needs.

12 BUILDING A POWERFUL SALES DEPARTMENT

"If you think it's expensive to hire a professional to do the job, wait until you hire an amateur."
Red Adair, Innovator and Legendary Oil Well Firefighter

In reviewing the development of a sales department, we identified a number of achievements that had been accomplished. From an overall sales perspective, the company grew from a high of £40,000 per month four years ago to over £250,000 in one month this year. The company is working with much larger individual client account volumes, and has competed for and secured large tendered work.

In order to keep up with this large volume of sales, Louise has been building a strong sales department by hiring both outside sales representatives and inside salespeople. Furthermore, she initiated a two-month training process for all new salespeople to help them orient to their new jobs and to the company before sending them into the field. This "training first" approach has been integrated into other departments in the company with good success.

Along the way, Louise has discovered and overcome a number of myths and misconceptions about building a strong sales department and hiring the right salespeople.

UNDERSTANDING THE NINE PRIMARY ROLES WITHIN SALES

> **Myth: If you want to grow your sales,**
> **just hire a good outside salesperson.**

"Michael," said Louise, "I was surprised with how our sales department has been evolving. As you know, before we started growing the company, it was either Kate or me handling the sales of the company," she said. "I thought that we would be finding and adding other outside sales reps, like me and Kate. I just naturally assumed that this was the way to go."

"This is a very common assumption," I told her. "When we think of salespeople, we generally think of the stereotypical outside sales rep. We don't even think of the other types of positions that constitute sales. However, there are many different types of sales roles, and each role requires looking for a different type of person."

> **Perspective Shift: Understand the different types**
> **of sales roles and clarify which type(s) would be**
> **best for your company.**

There are at least nine primary roles within sales. In addition to this, there are over a hundred permutations and derivations within sales organizations throughout the world. Here is a brief overview of each of the main categories.

1. Inside Sales - Outbound Calls

The outbound calling people are generally the "smiling and dialing" type. These are our telemarketers. They go through hundreds of "cold calls" or "semi-cold" leads each week, seeking to book appointments for more senior personnel.

2. Inside Sales - Inbound Call Acceptance

Inbound salespeople quite often take orders from customers calling in with requests. These are very common in industries with high volumes and much repeat work from the same customers.

3. New Business Development - Lead Generation

People in New Business Development–Lead Generation roles are often asked to seek out and develop initial relationships with potential customers, with the view of bringing in more technically skilled specialists later in the process. Similar to the telemarketers, there may be calling involved, but there is usually some market research done to pinpoint potential (usually large) opportunities.

4. Retail Sales

These people are found anywhere there is a store location or a mall, where the customers come to the business rather than the other way around. Roles within retail sales vary widely, ranging anywhere from the checkout people at the convenience store, right up to high-end vehicle and furniture sales. The role of the retail salesperson is to "serve" (read "sell to and service") new and existing customers.

5. Outside Salesperson - New Customer Acquisition

The person in this role is brought in to do one thing—to get new customers. The biggest differentiator here is the source of leads. Sometimes the role is based upon leads generated by the company, and other times the requirement is for the salesperson to source their own leads. However, the fundamental goal is to bring in more business from new customers.

6. Outside Sales - Existing Customer Retention

In addition to the salespeople who get new business from new customers, there are those who are hired to serve and support an existing customer base with repeat sales and ongoing support. They need to maintain, nurture, and grow existing customer relationships to keep their clientele happy and purchasing regularly.
It is not unusual for a salesperson to be expected to fill the roles of new customer acquisition as well as retaining existing customers that have been previously acquired.

7. Outside Sales and Project Management

The element that distinguishes this individual is that in addition to selling the business, this salesperson is responsible for participating in the delivery of goods and/or services to the customer.

8. Outside Sales - Territory Reps

One hybrid between types 5 and 6 above is the territory rep. That is, a person who is given a particular territory (either geographic or by industry sector) on an exclusive basis and is expected to serve and support existing customers as well as sell to new customers within that territory. Repeated contact over a period of time and regular "routes" or "circuits" are often developed as part of this role. The travelling salesperson is often a territory rep.

9. Sales and Public Relations

This role is a little different from the others. While people who fill this role develop contacts and relationships, there is no actual "selling." These people provide information to prospective clients on a regular basis in the hope that when that prospective client needs products or services, that salesperson's company will be chosen. Examples include pharmaceutical reps and travel agents.

"Louise, when you and Kate were bringing in all the new business, how would you classify your sales roles?" I asked.

"When we were smaller, we were a combination of your sales roles numbers 5, 6, and 7," she said. "We were working to get new customers, and we were dealing with repeat sales from our existing customers. Once we added project managers, we spent more of our time on 5 and 6, though we still keep an eye on our client projects."

"How were you getting your leads?" I asked her. "Were you sourcing them directly through your own networking and contacts, or did you have a lead generation system of some sort?"

"We were getting some from the different trade shows and conferences we attended," she responded. "However, most new projects came from either previous clients or from the online inquiries we got from our website. We weren't going out and drumming up business, except by staying in contact with our current clients."

"When did you decide you needed to grow your sales team?" I asked.

"I looked at hiring a new salesperson within six months of starting our plan to grow the company. Kate didn't really want to spend all her time being a salesperson, even though she is very good at sales. She knew the company would need a Creative Director and she wanted to grow into that type of role instead. That's really when I knew we had to find another salesperson. It was initially to replace Kate in the field."

Hiring outside salespeople is really a different exercise from hiring for other positions. The role of an outside salesperson is unique.

Finding a Strong Outside Salesperson

"When we started bringing on other salespeople," said Louise, "I thought for sure that we needed people who could generate their own leads. After all, that has been my picture of what a good salesperson should do."

"But that's not how you and Kate got your leads," I observed.

"No, we didn't," she said, "but I thought we needed more. There were only so many leads coming from the website, and shows only came around at certain points in the year. If we could find a new salesperson to find leads and win the business, we would be in good shape.

"So, we brought on someone who we thought could generate leads and also sell to those people. We identified some sectors where we have been successful and tried to steer the first person we hired, Brad [not his real name] in that direction.

"It didn't work too well with Brad. But I was not sure whether it was the job itself—were we asking one person to do too much?—or the fact that we may have picked the wrong person.

"I didn't know whether an outside salesperson who could also generate new leads was out there. Brad seemed to be struggling, but I was concerned it might be him."

"You also tried bringing in an inside sales support person shortly after that," I commented.

"Well," she said, "in the meantime, I also needed some help with my own sales, because I was being spread too thin. I was taking care of my own clients as well as supporting the managers as they grew in their various roles. We hired Kelly B as an Internal Solutions Advisor, effectively helping Kate and me with our workload and taking on some of the smaller inquiries.

TRAIN AND ORIENT YOUR SALESPEOPLE FIRST

> **Myth: Get salespeople going faster by getting them into the market as soon as possible.**

Normally, when we hire salespeople, we get them into the field as quickly as possible, knowing that they often take three to six months to get themselves established. That is consistent with conventional wisdom. The point that we miss is that during the first couple of months, new salespeople are getting themselves familiar with both the new company and the sales positioning of their new employer. As a result, no matter how good they are, it still takes time to become fully familiar with the new employer.

With this being true, there is very little, if anything lost by investing that first two months in training new salespeople on all aspects of their new company. In fact, investing this time in increasing the knowledge and comfort of salespeople with the company's systems, processes, and unique advantages holds a definite advantage.

"I learned a valuable lesson," said Louise. "I was always told that with salespeople, you get them going faster by getting them into the market as soon as possible.

"However, something very interesting happened with Kelly B. She had good sales experience, but she didn't have any experience in our industry. At your suggestion, Michael, we gave her two months of training and familiarizing herself with what we do in each of our departments before we allowed her to deal with any leads of her own.

"This was the strategy that Andrea had employed with Rachel when she joined our project management department without any elearning background. Even though she had plenty of project management experience, Andrea had Rachel invest two months in assisting the other PMs, while she learned about our industry and company. This gave Rachel the time to really excel. Now she is an excellent project manager for us.

"So when you and I talked about it, Michael, I agreed to try the same thing with Kelly B."

> **Perspective Shift: Take the time to train salespeople—even experienced people—while keeping them out of the field for one to two months.**

Louise went on to explain. "We started by having her spend time with each production group in the office: the instructional designers, the graphic designers and illustrators, the developers, and the project managers. We also had Kelly B. conduct a number of customer satisfaction surveys, to experience directly how our clients felt about the work that we did.

"In the meantime, I was getting Kelly B to help with proposals, and guiding her through our process by doing legwork for me on some of our current work. She also went out with me sometimes and with Kate as well on some of our new potential client calls, so she got to see the whole experience first-hand, without any pressure to sell on her own.

"That seemed to make a big difference in her development as a salesperson. In the third month, we gave Kelly B leads of her own to deal with, and by the end of that third month, she had sold more than Brad had sold in his first six months with us."

"But didn't Brad have the expertise and experience in the industry?" I asked.

"Yes, he did," Louise confirmed. "I figured at that point that maybe I had just hired the wrong person in Brad. I finally let him go after he had been with us for a year without really making any substantive progress."

> **Myth: If something doesn't work, don't try it again. That's just a waste of time, effort, and money.**

"I must admit, Michael, that when Brad didn't work out I got a bit disillusioned. To go back out to try another outside salesperson was tough. I was concerned that it was a waste of time, effort, and money."

"So, what made the difference?" I asked her, knowing she had moved past this concern.

"You brought up a really good point in one of the conversations that we had," she replied. "You suggested that we design the development of our sales department like a big experiment."

> **Perspective Shift: Give yourself permission to experiment, risk-manage your investment, and learn from your mistakes.**

As business owners, we spend a lot of time trying to avoid mistakes. Many of us feel that giving ourselves permission to experiment is really just a way to either justify or to cover up expensive mistakes. There is a different way to deal with it all.

When we are growing, we are bound to hit areas that are unknown to us. Being new to running a sales team, owners are not sure what to expect.

With Sponge and elearning, I wasn't quite sure what to expect either. Each industry is different. Everything about this business is online. After all, the company builds online training for its clients. So a natural assumption would be that customers would find the company from online sources.

However, some of Sponge's leads had been coming from traditional sources, like trade shows and referrals. There were a number of successful salespeople in this industry, so I figured there had to be a way that included some traditional approaches. We just needed to manage Louise's risk, so that she would have the staying power to go through the learning curve she needed to have this area of the business grow properly.

Trying a salesperson who doesn't work out can cost up to six months of wages, often with little, if anything, to show for it. The only way to stay sane in this is to acknowledge the risk, and then to put a cap or limit on how much to spend while experimenting.

"That's exactly what we did," Louise said. "We decided to cap the risk at the equivalent of six months' wages for any individual salesperson, and then to limit our exposure to the equivalent of one person's wage at a time. If someone sold enough to cover one of the six months, that person got an extension of another month, and so on.

"One thing you pointed out to me that helped me with this was to see how much gross profit each person was generating, and what were their monthly wages. By comparing those two numbers, it gave me more patience to let things evolve and see how they worked out. Even if they weren't hitting the goals we wanted, as long as they were covering their costs, we had time to let things unfold.

"Even though Brad wasn't selling enough, at least he was covering his costs plus a bit. So it didn't cost me more money to keep him than he was bringing in, at least not if you ignore our training and support time. I treated that time as an additional investment I was willing to make.

"Once we saw some success with Kelly B, we used the extra gross profit to invest in the next person. By using this staged approach, the salespeople were covering themselves and each other. I found it much easier to experiment by using this risk-management strategy. It allowed me to settle in and discover what I needed to learn, and to really understand what works for us.

"Had I not done that, I might have shrunk back to a level that Kate and I could sell, and not continued to grow. That strategy made a big difference to our whole growth plan," she said. "It helped when Kelly B started succeeding. That told me that these experiments were definitely worth the risk."

The Experiment Continues

Knowing that Brad wasn't working out, and in line with continuing to experiment, Louise next tried the outside sales route again, by hiring David [not his real name] who was also an experienced veteran.

David had a lot more going for him than Brad had. Hiring Brad was just a mistake. The fit wasn't there and he wasn't very good at sales, despite his own claims to the contrary.

By contrast, the company didn't have that problem with Kelly B at all. She did need some help with developing the appropriate solutions, so either Kate or Louise would step in and help her there. It also took her a while to get some of the nuances of the proposal process, but that came within a few months. And when she did make a mistake, she was mortified and vowed to never make it again. She grew very quickly. Louise found that to be a far more pleasant experience than it was to deal with Brad, who would justify his mistakes, and make excuses.

"Let's go back to David," I suggested.

"He was a seasoned pro and expected to be paid like one," said Louise. "He wanted even more than I was paying Brad, which was a lot. I agreed to a much higher base salary as well as commissions.

"At least David came to the table with a plan for how much he would sell in the first year. Even though I had been asking for this from Brad, he never did manage to provide it. I thought David's plan was a bit low for the amount of money I was paying him, but I could also see the logic in it, and there was planned growth built in for year two, so I agreed."

"How did it go with him?" I asked.

"Two things happened," she said. "First, he was always asking about how we could get him more leads. When I hired him, I told him that I would be providing some leads, but that I was expecting him to find his own leads over time. Once on board, he kept complaining that he didn't have enough people to talk to. He did do some networking, and he did drum up a few leads, but nothing that panned out.

"We didn't have a robust marketing department then, but we eventually hired Emma, our marketing manager, to do some marketing research and coordination. We were hopeful that more leads would be coming soon. The problem I was having was that David was getting the same number of leads as Kelly B. She was bringing in results from her leads. And with what I gave David, he wasn't producing.

"Finally, since David was underperforming to even his conservative projections with company-fed leads with no realistic sense that he would improve, I let him go, too."

"How long did that take?" I asked.

"I let him go after six months," Louise replied. "I'm getting faster at dealing with these situations when they don't work."

She smiled. "And I didn't exceed the cap I had set for that experiment," she added. "He did bring in a couple of small deals while he worked with us."

"If you had it to do again, would have done anything differently?" I asked.

Louise said, "I would have probably tried spending the same one to two months training David on our ways before getting him to go in the field. Though, in his case, I'm not sure it would have made a difference."

"Why is that?" I questioned.

"He was a seasoned salesperson. He thought he knew everything already, so I doubt if he would let in much, if any, training. I just have that feeling about him."

"Is this something you could have picked up through the selection process, back when you were hiring him?" I asked.

Louise thought about this for a moment.

"Yes, I could have" she finally said. "Thinking back, I can now see it a mile away. I just didn't know that this type of attitude was an impediment to effectiveness in sales. I was looking for someone who was sociable and outgoing. That's what I thought people needed to be like to be good at sales."

HIRING EFFECTIVE SALESPEOPLE

> **Misconception: People need to be sociable and outgoing to be good at sales.**

"Believing this is what had me a bit surprised by the extent of Kelly B's success," admitted Louise. "And seeing her success is what dispelled me from that belief. She is a very nice and friendly person, but I wouldn't call her outgoing. She is very quiet and professional, not your backslapping, jovial sales type at all. Yet she outperformed Brad, and subsequently David, who were both more outgoing."

> **Perspective Shift: Effective salespeople come in all the different personality types, just like the rest of us.**

It seems that we have these preconceived notions of what a successful salesperson looks like, how they act, how they deal with people, and so on. This comes from TV, the movies, and books that feed certain stereotypes.

In truth, salespeople, both effective and ineffective, come in all shapes and sizes, and with different types of personalities. There are introverts, extroverts, noisy, quiet, old, young, tall, short, fat, thin ... you get the picture. Personality and physical attributes are not what marks a good salesperson.

"At the start of this journey, we had no experience in hiring people," said Louise. "Then, when we learned how to hire people to add to our staff, I figured that hiring salespeople would be just like hiring other staff," she said.

> **Myth: Hiring salespeople is just like hiring other staff.**

Even though they may come in all shapes, sizes, and personalities, salespeople are quite different from other people, sometimes in subtle ways. Salespeople are a different breed, and need to be sought out and hired differently from the normal way of hiring people.

> **Perspective Shift: Hiring salespeople is not the same as hiring for other roles within a company.**

Each role within a company is designed to achieve either one or both of two distinct functions.

Two Core Functions of All Staff

To be effective within a company, everyone in the company needs to be focused on either:

- maintaining or enhancing the customer's experience of value, or
- protecting and enhancing the company's profit.

In some roles, they do both. Those are the two elements of the value exchange. Salespeople often have additional roles.

Salesperson as Keeper of the Client's Experience of Value

The salesperson's role is rather unique, since this person starts that client relationship and sets the tone for the client's experience of value. A valuable salesperson often acts as the face of the company, and has a huge influence on the company's reputation. How this person handles clients and customers will have a dramatic impact on their experience of the company, both at the start of the relationship, and as things unfold over time.

As an example, let's take Kate at Sponge UK. She follows up a lead that was provided, based on a trade show, a web inquiry, or a referral from an existing client. Kate's job is to introduce the company, and then listen actively for the goals, needs, and concerns of the potential client. Then she is involved in coming up with potential alternative approaches and a plan for clients, with pricing and terms, as well as timing for client deliverables.

A project manager, an instructional designer, and a graphic designer all get involved with the client's project. Kate will also continue to be part of the picture, supporting the client along the way, sometimes also helping the project manager to get what is needed from the client so that the company can meet its commitments on a timely basis.

Even with the project manager's involvement, salespeople like Kate have a very large impact on how the company is perceived by clients. They set the tone for the relationship, and then nurture it along the way.

Salesperson as Protector of Company Profit

Kate's job in sales doesn't stop there. She is also responsible to ensure the profitability of the work she quotes. There is a balance between pricing a project low enough to ensure securing the work, and pricing the project high enough to ensure a profit.

In the case of most senior salespeople (such as Kate), this is also a responsibility that they accept as part of their role.

Salesperson as Lead Generator – Enhancing Company Profit

In situations where salespeople need to identify and secure their own leads, there is another dimension present. These people need to initiate relationships in the marketplace that may not have previously existed. Whether it is through providing speeches in public, signing up for and attending trade shows, networking, or doing any of a multitude of strategies, salespeople who generate their own leads become marketers as well.

Turning Potential Into Reality

One of the biggest differences that define salespeople is that their job includes converting a potential customer into a real one. Instead of being someone who may buy our goods and services, the customer turns into someone who actually makes the purchase.

TOP TEN ATTRIBUTES OF AN EFFECTIVE SALESPERSON

As a result of all this, there are distinct criteria for hiring an outside salesperson that are fairly consistent among differing companies, but fairly unique to sales.

Let's start with the list of six A-Player criteria that we referred to when hiring for anyone in the company. We want people who:

- are positive,
- are resourceful,
- have a bias for action,
- are strong at completion,
- anticipate well, and
- look to contribute.

These attributes are very important for salespeople, just as they are for anyone else in the company. In addition, here is a list of ten additional criteria to use when selecting people to add to an outside sales team.

1. Drive and ambition: the will to win – Salespeople are paid to generate specific, measurable results: new clients and customers for the company. Sometimes this can be daunting, especially in the face of people telling them "No" a lot. None of us likes to be told No. This internal drive of the salesperson is what overcomes the hesitation associated with the Noes so that they keep going and generate the Yeses, and sales success.

2. Exceptional listening skill – The skill of listening may be the most important attribute that is possessed by strong salespeople. Without the ability to listen and hear at depth, clients won't be truly understood, and solutions won't match client needs as well, resulting in reduced effectiveness and performance.

3. Natural curiosity: ask-oriented – This is linked to point number 2. There seem to be two types of salespeople. Those who ask, and those who tell. If I tell, I become a pitchman. If I ask, I will find out more. Associated with this is a natural curiosity. If I have a healthy dose of curiosity, I will naturally be inclined to ask more, find out more, and be better informed when it comes to solving client needs.

4. Big picture view – This attribute is just as important to sales as it is to management. To be a top manager, I need to be able to see how the skills and talents of different people come together to give me the coordinated performance that will deliver the department objectives. In sales, it is a bit different. I need to understand where my product fits into the client's situation, and how it might integrate to provide the client with the maximum result. Without the depth of perspective that comes with the big picture view, I will definitely be limited in my growth as a salesperson.

5. Good at articulating clearly – As the primary ambassador of the company, if I can't articulate clearly, I just won't be understood, which will adversely impact my ability to sell.

6. Fundamental respect for people – I have seen salespeople who don't respect others. Some of them actually do okay, but they are clearly limited and generally don't maximize their effectiveness. It is only through this level of respect that an authentic connection can be made, maintained, and strengthened over time. Growing connections over time adds to the effectiveness of anyone in sales.

7. Well-centered sense of self – The more grounded a person I am, the more effective I will be in whatever I do. This is amplified in sales, where I am constantly interacting with others. While this evolves over time, as salespeople gain a stronger sense of self, magically results improve.

8. Courage – at two levels

1. **The courage to actively and continually step into the unknown** – Effective outside salespeople are consistently opening new doors, without knowing what is behind them. This takes courage, a facility to deal with the unknown and a comfort level with uncertainty.
2. **The courage to say what needs to be said** – Many of us are just a little bit (or a lot) chicken to tell the truth to someone. We are afraid that they won't like us, nor will they buy from us. This is normal. Yet, in many cases, clients need and appreciate someone who points out what they are missing. This takes courage. Yet, it is instrumental to increased sales success, especially in more complex sales.

9. Strong discernment – It is one thing to have courage to speak out, and another to have the good judgment to know when to speak and when to stay silent. That is all part of strong discernment.

10. Eager to learn and grow – The profession of sales is constantly changing. An openness to learn is insufficient these days. Without an active eagerness to learn and grow, people get passed over. True enduring effectiveness has ongoing learning as a core element.

"These criteria have really assisted us in the growth of our sales department," Louise commented. "Jason, our latest hire for the outside sales position, has all these attributes, and he is flourishing with us. I am really pleased with his progress.

"Trudie is our newest addition in this department. She is still learning and growing in the role, so she hasn't had a chance to show us what she has yet, but so far, so good," Louise added.

"Overall, Louise, how would you say you have done with the development of your sales department?" I asked her.

"It has had its ups and downs," she replied. "But overall, I am quite satisfied. I have learned a great deal, and I am learning more every day. I think it is progressing well. It goes hand-in-hand with the growth of our marketing department," she added.

I responded, "That's where we are going next."

Summary of Myths and Misconceptions

1. Myth: If you want to grow your sales, just hire a good outside salesperson.
2. Myth: Get salespeople going faster by getting them into the market as soon as possible.
3. Myth: If something doesn't work, don't try it again. That's just a waste of time, effort, and money.
4. Misconception: People need to be sociable and outgoing to be good at sales.
5. Myth: Hiring salespeople is just like hiring other staff.

Summary of Perspective Shifts

1. Understand the different types of sales roles, and clarify which type(s) would be best for your company.
2. Take the time to train salespeople—even experienced people—while keeping them out of the field for one to two months.
3. Give yourself permission to experiment, risk-manage your investment, and learn from your mistakes.
4. Effective salespeople come in all the different personality types, just like the rest of us.
5. Hiring salespeople is not the same as hiring for other roles within a company.

Tools in this Chapter

1. The Nine Primary Roles within Sales

1. Inside Sales – Outbound Calls
2. Inside Sales – Inbound Call Acceptance
3. New Business Development – Lead Generation
4. Retail Sales
5. Outside Sales – New Customer Acquisition
6. Outside Sales – Existing Customer Retention
7. Outside Sales and Project Management
8. Outside Sales – Territory Reps
9. Sales and Public Relations

2. Top Ten Attributes of Effective Outside Salespeople

1. Drive and ambition: the will to win
2. Exceptional listening skill
3. Natural curiosity: Ask-oriented
4. Big picture view
5. Good at articulating clearly
6. Fundamental respect for people
7. Well-centered sense of self
8. Courage – at two levels
9. Strong discernment
10. Eager to learn and grow

13 THE EVOLUTION OF A MARKETING STRATEGY

"Selling to people who actually want to hear from you is more effective than interrupting strangers who don't."
Seth Godin, best-selling author, entrepreneur, and public speaker

Sponge's marketing has been evolving in a number of ways that are turning out to be significant. The company had been getting six to twelve leads per week from Google AdWords without anyone in a marketing department. This was just considered a lead generation strategy for Louise and Kate, as the company's two initial salespeople. Over the past year, with the addition of new salespeople, they increased their spending and bumped the leads to twenty-four per week.

In 2013, Louise hired Emma as marketing manager to do basic research and help Sponge with the legwork to support outside sales reps with lead generation in specific sectors. Emma has since been actively growing her own marketing team.

We clarified what work had been done in which sectors (sorted by types of projects) and cross-referenced these within the sectors the company had been serving. Louise, Kate, and Emma conducted customer satisfaction surveys to clarify a number of different things about clients, their buying habits, and their needs for elearning.

Louise knew the strategic significance of good information. Working with Emma, she analyzed the business to determine the levels of repeat business they received, as well as client Lifetime Value (LTV). From there Louise worked with Emma to start to build out sector-based marketing and lead generation strategies (beginning with Pharma). As part of this, Louise hired Phil, an industry expert, to help unfold the Pharma strategy for Jason.

With the rebranding project complete, which helped position Sponge with a new, fresh look, the company's work in the four trade shows per year has continued to generate stronger and stronger results. In fact, Louise has become a featured speaker at some of these conferences.

In a very short time (since November 2013) the marketing department has moved from nonexistent to a major force in the company.

MARKETING STRATEGY: GETTING STARTED

Louise started the conversation.

"Michael, before I considered adding a whole marketing department, I thought that it was only something that big companies had. We were just selling to our customers, so why would we need marketing? Kate and I attended the tradeshows and conferences where a presence would help us. Some leads were coming in from our website. I thought we were too small to use marketing."

> **Misconception: We are too small to use marketing.**

This is a common misconception. Due to perceived costs of advertising and other marketing initiatives, many of us think that we need to be bigger to formally start building marketing into our organizations. Marketing, like finance and administration, doesn't directly get new deals (like sales), nor does it produce products or services (like operations). So while we are aware that there must be benefits of having people on staff supporting our business development efforts, owners often think that the size of the company has to be much bigger and that building a marketing department is something to be done at that later time. Otherwise, why add the overhead?

"Is that still what you think?" I asked.

"No," she replied. "If we do it properly, marketing is a highly strategic part of our business."

> **Perspective Shift: Done properly, marketing is a strategic part of the business.**

Louise has been developing the marketing department and learning new places where the people in this part of the company can help everyone. Marketing, in its own quiet way, is having a big impact on the growth of the company. The experiments in the sales department have had a real chance at success, due to the efforts of a growing marketing team who are actively generating more new leads. Growing the number of leads that the company is attracting and achieving each salesperson's goals for new sales go hand-in-hand. The people in marketing are handling all that now, on a dedicated basis.

"Michael," said Louise, "when we started to develop our marketing strategy, my initial thoughts were to better understand our market, our competitors, and how we were different. I thought that was where we should start. When I was reading books on business plans that is where they suggested people start in building a marketing strategy."

> **Misconception: The place to start in developing a marketing strategy is to understand our market, our competitors, and how we are different from them.**

Almost every traditional marketing book I have read starts people here—examining their market and competitors. This is smart for big businesses, where there are many things to sort through to clarify the ideal market, especially in differing geographic climates. Yet a small to medium sized business is very different from a big business.

In a small business, the biggest threat is time. There is too much to do and too little in terms of personnel resources to do it. As a result, "nice to have" exercises, while they may have some value, waste more time than they save. There is still legwork to do, but let's make sure that it is highly useful information, not factoids, that won't move us forward substantially.

"Michael, you had us start in a different place," said Louise. "You recommended that we carry out marketing surveys with our clients."

"Yes," I said. "Traditional business plans in big businesses may need to clarify their potential market. Yet business plans for smaller companies are mostly designed to help business owners justify and secure funding, either from lenders (the banks) or from investors. These people want to know that you understand your market and where you fit within that market. This gives them increased peace of mind to invest with or lend to you.

"That was not your purpose in developing a marketing

strategy. You just wanted to grow your business, and you wanted a direction to take to do that. For this purpose, in my opinion, always start marketing efforts by focusing on your clients and customers. The more you understand them from their perspective, the more likely you will be to attract more of them to your company. Your biggest asset is your customer database, but only if it is bursting with relevant information."

> **Perspective Shift: Always start marketing efforts by focusing on your clients and customers.**

A highly effective method to initiating a marketing strategy is to ensure that we understand everything about the people who already pay us money for the privilege of working with us. This takes time, but the returns are invaluable!

Some people, like Louise, are concerned at the start, wondering whether their clients and customers would be willing to share information about themselves, as well as their experiences with the company. Very few of us like surveys. However, we feel important if our suppliers check in with us to see how they are doing, and how they might improve for us. This changes acceptance relatively easily.

"At the start," said Louise, "I was a bit worried about how well the clients would take to answering questions about us. We are all busy people. But your strategy worked well. Over a period of two months, we carried out fifteen surveys, which revealed critical information about what clients liked about our services and where we could improve. Kate and I found that information really useful. The surveys didn't take too long to do, usually about twenty minutes each, but clients valued being heard.

"Once this work was completed, we prepared a Marketing Messages Worksheet and a Lifetime Value Analysis sheet.

(see Table 1) It helped us notice patterns and gain a deeper understanding of our clients' issues.

Table 1: Sponge Marketing Messages Worksheet and Lifetime Value Analysis

	Client A	Client B	Client C
Lifetime Value	**$150,000**	**$80,000**	**$400,000**
Symptom - fear	Risks associated with non- compliance of the equality act which could see employees and the company fined and damage their reputation if breached	Fear of employee litigation due to managers not being aware of or following the best practice HR guidelines.	Inability of new employees to communicate and protect the company's values, vision, and goals due to lack of awareness and understanding.
General need	To ensure compliance with an external regulation for all employees and to remain compliant year on year.	Training managers in new HR guidelines.	The need is awareness training in company values, vision, and goals for new employees.
Specific requirement	Suite of legal compliance modules	Suite of HR modules for managers based on the latest guidelines and policies	Induction which also addresses quality issues and how the company dealt with them
What we do now	Wrote, designed, and built modules. Organized a video shoot.	Wrote, designed, and built modules using guidelines and policies and bringing these to life with scenarios and interactions	Wrote, designed, and built module based on their training presentations, brand guidelines, and videos.
What we could do	Refresher modules. Feedback surveys to measure effectiveness. Mobile apps to view video lessons.	Feedback survey to measure effectiveness and determine if more elearning is needed. Mobile apps for social care workers. Blended learning solutions- training/ workshop packs for facilitators	Trailer to promote it. 3-D simulations. Mobile apps to make it more accessible. Sales skills modules.
Client benefits	They can provide to their staff compliance modules for peace of mind. Could do annual refreshers so they don't have to do it all again every year. Make it more accessible through mobile apps	Consistent HR training is now available for HR managers. More targeted and effective elearning. Make it more accessible through mobile apps.	Employees have a comprehensive induction. There would be more take-up if better promoted and more accessible.

"This exercise helped us to reflect on and define our ideal clients," she added.

MARKETING STRATEGY: IDENTIFYING THE IDEAL CLIENT

Information about existing and previous clients can assist us greatly in identifying who we want to attract as new clients. There are clients with whom we have had really rewarding experiences, and then there are others who just cost us money. In looking at a number of variables of what we liked or didn't like about our various existing or previous clients, we may then develop a profile of who would make the ideal client, for us.

Louise's Observations on Clarifying the Company's Ideal Client

"Michael," said Louise, "at your suggestion, we developed five criteria to establish who we wanted to work with, and how we might help them. The ideal client:

1. is one we can bring value to on a sustainable basis.
2. is profitable (both tangible and intangible) for us.
3. works with us on a repeat and referral basis.
4. meets a profile.
5. helps us with other considerations."

Louise went on to explain the five criteria.

1. Is one we can bring value to on a sustainable basis

"The questions we ask ourselves here are:
- Does this give us an opportunity to fulfill their need using our unique ability (UA) / expertise?
- Do this client's projects give us an opportunity to grow our skills where we are strong or where we would like to develop further strength?
- Do they appreciate us and what we bring?

"For us, these are all needed to ensure that value is brought on a sustainable basis. If we are not being appreciated, or if we are not growing, we may do good and valuable work, but it won't be a sustainable relationship of continued value both ways. With the ideal client, we are bringing value, and getting the chance to continue to grow to be able to bring more value into the future.

2. Is profitable (both tangible and intangible) for us

"To be ideal for us, there are some things we need to consider:
- Will the project be delivered profitably within the desired margin and at the right price?
- Will they be quick to pay?
- Are they enjoyable to work with for our staff?
- Do they treat us like equals with expertise, or people to boss around?
- Are we happy to work with them?

"We work really hard for the benefit of our clients. We want to ensure that it is a good deal, both financially and non-financially for us too. There are two elements to profit for us. Tangible profits include being funded well enough to do a proper job, and being paid on a timely basis. Intangible profit is all about the working relationship. Is it fun to work with their people? If so, our people will gain from the experience, which is a form of intangible profit for us.

"If we hate working with a client, there is usually a disconnect at the level of core values somewhere, and we are better off just not working with them, than we are in making our staff miserable. Life is too short.

3. Works with us on a repeat and referral basis

"We ask ourselves whether a client is likely to have other needs into the future, in addition to the work being requested in the present. When we are really busy, if we have to say no to someone, we would rather not turn down people who have lots of potential projects coming up on an ongoing basis.

"The second question we ask is, "Will they refer us to other departments with similar values?" Many will. These are more ideal for us.

4. Meets a profile

"The ideal client for us meets one of a number of internal profiles we have of clients for whom we can do our best work. The questions we ask ourselves are:

- Will their brand enhance our portfolio?
- Does this client fit into one of the profiles where we can do our best work?

5. Helps us with other considerations

"From time to time, there are other considerations, such as:

- Does this client give us an opportunity to provide work when we are not busy, filling downtime?
- Does this client have flexibility of timing when we are super busy?
- How easy is it to work with them and make (and keep) them happy?

"By thinking about this and describing in detail who our ideal client was helped us when new enquiries came in. Do they meet our ideal client profile? We don't want to work with everyone. Just those that are the right fit for us and we are the right fit for our clients," Louise concluded.

MARKETING STRATEGY: BUILDING A MARKETING TEAM

In November 2013, Emma joined Sponge as marketing manager. This was a big move for Louise and her team, as before they didn't really do any marketing, or so she thought. Their enquiries came through the website, which was great, but the company was also being reactive rather than choosing the markets they wanted to be experts in. When Louise hired Emma, she expected immediate results. Why else, she thought, would she pay someone that just costs the company overhead?

> **Misconception: Marketing takes effect immediately.**

Emma started writing press releases, blogs, actively using social media, and took on overseeing the pay-per-click Google marketing. She investigated other trade shows, organized webinars for the company to run, and arranged public speaking events. After eight months, Louise began to see the benefits of the marketing with the company's monthly incoming leads doubling. One thing she started to realize was that marketing activity really takes effect six to twelve months later.

> **Perspective Shift: Marketing activity takes effect six to twelve months later.**

Given the company's sales forecasts for the next twelve months, Louise knew it was going to be necessary to bolster the marketing team. She decided to take on a PR specialist who could write more in-depth articles and a graduate to help Emma with events. Within a short period of ten months, Louise had a department of three and was recruiting for an online marketing specialist to cover all their bases.

> **Myth: Only build the marketing team consistent with our current size.**

A common myth we see in action is to invest in a marketing team only to the size of current operations. Here's the problem with that. A marketing department in a growing company serves one primary goal—to generate growth. To size the marketing department to the "current" company size is a mistake.

Having enough people to handle current business will keep the current business activities flowing, but without additional resources in this department, it is almost impossible to grow substantially. To be strategic with the marketing department, the marketing team today should reflect the intended size of the company one to three years from now.

> **Perspective Shift: The marketing team today should reflect the intended size of the company one to three years from now.**

To attract the business that you need today takes effort. To grow the business to the point that you envision one, two, or three years down the road, will take even more effort. Investment in the team and resources needed to be in place now so that it can support tomorrow's size, not today's. This is another version of "hire ahead of the curve."

MARKETING STRATEGY: PUTTING THE MARKETING TEAM TO WORK

Myth: Marketing is all about new clients.

A very common myth that we fall into as business owners is to merely think about new clients when we think of the marketing department. We figure that the salespeople will keep relationships strong with existing or previous clients. This is a logical thought, and sometimes it is valid. Yet, more often than not, existing and previous clients slip between the cracks. Further, far too few companies have organized referral systems in place.

The most lucrative source of new business comes from people who already deal with us. A properly functioning marketing department should be equipped to actively nurture and continue to grow these established relationships, not just the new ones.

Perspective Shift: Use the marketing team to support repeat business from existing and previous clients, not just new client acquisition.

We generally believe that repeat and referral business sits squarely in the domain of existing salespeople. It does sit there. Yet, salespeople are often under so much pressure to acquire new business that they sometimes forget to circle back to existing or previous clients, especially for periodic (non-regular) purchases. The marketing department can be instrumental in maximizing repeat and referral business from previous clients.

"Our rate of repeat business with existing clients is very high," said Louise. "Sometimes though, client needs are not immediate. We don't want our salespeople to overlook previous clients who need us again a year or two later. So, we have been developing a system to continue to support these people. This has been integrated into the marketing department. While it is still early days, I am confident that this initiative will allow us to serve our clients better."

"It is far easier to get more business from happy clients than it is to try to entice new clients who don't yet know you to buy from you," I mentioned.

To this, Louise agreed.

"Are there any other myths or misconceptions you had regarding marketing?" I asked.

"There is one," responded Louise. "I always thought that the marketing effort was only about clients and customers."

> **Misconception: The marketing effort is only about clients and customers.**

The marketing department can have a huge impact on recruiting high-calibre people into the company. The fact is that in addition to potential clients, the people who read company's website the most are usually potential employees. The marketing department is in a unique place to contribute in meaningful ways to attracting key staff, across all departments. Louise has discovered this fact.

"We talked about this a bit before," said Louise. "With our level of growth, I have discovered that we need to be treating the recruitment of staff as a marketing initiative."

> ## Perspective Shift: With high levels of growth, the recruitment of staff becomes a marketing initiative.

"If our company wants one new person in a department," said Louise, "we will typically follow standard protocols that we have in place to find this person. However, if we need ten staff within a six- to twelve-month window, we change how we look and what strategies we use. The strategies for larger numbers of staff are often marketing strategies.

"We have been working on a brochure to attract bright new staff. We are also setting plans in place to position some of our senior designers and developers as thought leaders in the industry, to help us become better known. This means hiring an online social media person who can also do PR, just for recruitment. When we need to bring on as many new people as we do to meet our goals for growth, this strategy makes great sense."

"Excellent!" I said. "I fully anticipate that by treating your recruitment activities as a marketing endeavor, you will be happy with the results."

"Is there anything else to review in this department?" I asked.

"No, that is pretty much where we sit," replied Louise.

"That completes our review of at least the main shifts that have occurred for you during these past few years. What is next is to look at, well, what's next!" I said. "Let's turn our focus to the future."

"This is the part that I have been looking forward to discussing," Louise commented. "Let's go!"

Summary of Myths and Misconceptions

1. Misconception: We are too small to use marketing.
2. Misconception: The place to start in developing a marketing strategy is to understand our market, our competitors, and how we are different from them.
3. Misconception: Marketing takes effect immediately.
4. Myth: Only build the marketing team consistent with our current size.
5. Myth: Marketing is all about new clients.
6. Misconception: The marketing effort is only about clients and customers.

Summary of Perspective Shifts

1. Done properly, marketing is a strategic part of the business.
2. Always start marketing efforts by focusing on your clients and customers.
3. Marketing activity takes effect six to twelve months later.
4. The marketing team today should reflect the intended size of the company one to three years from now.
5. Use the marketing team to support repeat business from existing and previous clients, not just new client acquisition.
6. With high levels of growth, the recruitment of staff becomes a marketing initiative.

Section 4: The Future

"*The bad news is time flies. The good news is you're the pilot.*"
Michael Altshuler, Entrepreneur and Motivational Speaker

14 WHERE TO FROM HERE?

"You have brains in your head. You have feet in your shoes.
You can steer yourself any direction you choose.
You're on your own. And you know what you know.
And YOU are the one who'll decide where to go ..."
Dr. Seuss, *Oh, The Places You'll Go!*

With the review of the main perspective shifts over the past three years completed, we next looked forward to the future. The goal that Louise shared with me is to bring the company from its current level of £2 million in revenues to £10 million within the next three to four years. She has already achieved a five-fold increase once, and she is confident that it can be done again. The people on her team are learning and growing, and her company is able to make a meaningful difference to more clients with wider reach than ever before.

"Louise," I asked, "what is prompting you to take your business to the next levels of growth? Aren't you satisfied with the size of company that you have already achieved?"

"I'm thrilled with what we have accomplished," she said. "But, I'm not done ... not by a long way."

"What's driving your passion to grow?"

Louise pondered this question before responding.

"When I was nine, I became quite fascinated by my father's family who lived in Greece. I was always intrigued with the letters that would arrive with strange Greek writing, and I became infatuated with going to Greece. Finally, after some gentle persuasion my father booked me a ticket to Greece to stay with my aunts, uncles, and cousins, even though we had never met.

"When I first arrived, I was terribly homesick, couldn't speak Greek, and wasn't too sure about the food. After four days of crying in bed, I decided that since I was there, I had better get on with it. I picked up my *Divry's English-Greek Dictionary* and began to learn the language with my cousins. A few weeks into my stay with my aunt's family, I had an amazing realization that there were families just like mine living all over the world who spoke different languages.

"Defining moments like these have stayed with me and have strongly influenced the shape of Sponge today. It seems natural to me that Sponge would go international—learning is not bound by borders. We translate our elearning into many languages around the world. The idea that people all over the world could be benefiting from our services is thrilling.

"One of my proudest moments was to win an international tender from the United Nations for an induction module for humanitarian workers based in remote places around the world. Later, we also won work with the United Nations International Fund for Agricultural Development, which helps support the rural poor."

"So that's why you want to go international," I commented.

"Yes," she said. Then Louise continued to explain.

"I fully plan on developing international offices. When we redesigned our logo after ten years, we decided to include 'UK' as part of our name with the plan to substitute this with EU and

USA when we have offices in Europe and the States or other regions we might consider.

"The second thing that drives me is clear to me as I see the growth of the people who work as part of our team. When I look at Kate, Alex, Alan, Andrea, and the others, I am amazed at how they have grown and matured in such a short period of time. These are people who are at least twenty years younger than me. They are taking life on and becoming much stronger people in the process. I want to keep growing this company to provide these people and others like them with the chance to learn, to grow, and discover what's possible for themselves and the contributions they can make for others.

"That leads to the third thing that is driving me to grow this business. I am having a great time! I feel alive and energized. I love coming to work every day. I'm certainly not ready to retire yet. After growing as much as we have, standing still now doesn't make a lot of sense. We are having too much fun, even through the chaos of fast-paced growth.

"The fourth thing driving me, but by no means the least, is the impact we are having on our clients and their people. In the work that we do, we have been growing our reach in supporting others. By providing elearning that absorbs, we are contributing in meaningful ways to the lives of hundreds of thousands of people. There is no reason we can't bring that number to millions of people trained and supported. I find that really exhilarating!"

"Don't things get difficult dealing with all the changes on a constant basis?" I asked.

"Yes, they do," Louise confirmed. "There are challenges, and even chaotic situations that come up fairly regularly, but that keeps us alert and aware."

Louise and her team have grown the company significantly over these past few years. She has worked through a number of areas, and has shifted her perspective on numerous aspects of business and business growth.

Yet, as she moves to the next level of growth, the game will change again. The balance points that were there before will once again go out the window, creating uncertainty and unpredictability for Louise and her people.

LOUISE'S OBSERVATIONS: NOTICING WHEN THE GAME CHANGES

"There are points in growth where the game changes," Louise observed. "The way we are doing things now needs to change quickly or we will slow down the growth process.

"Over the last year, we have been developing our sales team. We also rebranded the company and were doing much more marketing activity. Sales started to build and we were winning much bigger projects. In June, we achieved nearly a quarter of a million in sales in one month and the trend was continuing.

"Then in July and August, we had the problem of not enough staff to do the work. Managers were concerned about what might happen if they took more people on and the work slowed down. So they were hesitant to hire new staff. Yet at the same time, they were overwhelmed with the amount of work. The people on the sales team were reluctant to tell the project management team that they had won new sales, as they were so overworked.

"Michael," said Louise, "when you visited us in June you predicted this would occur and made it clear what needed to be done. We needed a big recruitment drive. We were soon to be understaffed in every department. This happened just as you suggested, with staff in danger of burnout. This meant hiring twenty-one new people between June and the end of the year.

"You also said that as a business, we were retaining too much profit and needed to invest in more staff. When you said that, I realized the game had changed. It was so ingrained in me to retain profit and be careful with recruiting. I hadn't really noticed the game had changed by so much. It took a good month for me to understand why we needed to recruit so many people, but when we analyzed it and went through it department by department it made sense. Despite this, I can't deny, at the time it seemed scary."

Michael's Observations: Growth at the Next Level

Louise and her people had worked diligently to achieve the gains they had accomplished. Yet things were still "lumpy" between sales and production. They had really strong sales in June and July, which sent a big swell of projects through their system from July through October. They have had difficulties keeping up with the project work, while also attracting and hiring the right people for their respective teams within the company.

How do we, as business owners, keep planting the seeds for future business that will pay for all the additional staff we need to deliver on our promises? What level of investment in more people is appropriate at any point in time?

The problem is that the balance point keeps changing through different levels of growth.

After taking some time to absorb the new reality of growth at the next level, Louise jumped in. Instead of continuing with "reasonable" efforts to attract new staff (a slow process at the best of times), she hired a recruiter and is now in the process of growing the internal recruiting team to three people: two recruiters and a human resources assistant.

The company is also actively using recruiting firms to find the right people, both in their own geographic area and in different parts of the UK, as well as other countries. As Sponge is only hiring new people who fit with both the job and embrace the company's core values, they need to go through more potential applicants to find the right fit.

They are making steady progress. Between August and December, they have grown by the twenty-one people they wanted, reaching their staff goal of fifty by year's end.

INTERNATIONAL RECOGNITION

The company has definitely achieved major levels of progress that have been felt internally and acknowledged both externally and internationally. As the year 2014 wound up, Sponge UK won Gold Medal for Elearning Development Company of the Year, the highest international award in that industry.[10]

THE FUTURE: PREPARING FOR GROWTH AT A WHOLE NEW LEVEL

That elusive balance point associated with growth continues to shift as the company grows. Louise has felt the effect of those spinning plates in all areas of her business, while dealing with the shifting market realities that continue to occur. She, Kate, and Matt have realized that if they want to grow to £10 million—another five-fold increase—within the next three to four years, they have to treat the next level of growth as if they are starting from scratch.

They have already broken through a number of myths and misconceptions that stop business growth and have a much better idea of what to expect. Louise is far more grounded in the reality of what is available, and she is clear that they will achieve the goal they are setting for the growth of Sponge.

---

[10]Source:www.trainingpressreleases.com/news/sponge/2014/sponge-uk-named-elearning -company-of-the-year

REGAINING BALANCE AS THE COMPANY GROWS: SEVEN AREAS OF FOCUS

Even though Louise is confident about the company's future, she is also clear that she will continue to run into more myths and misconceptions that will threaten her company's plans for growth. During the current intense recruiting effort, she has been feeling the impact of that balance point of the spinning plates changing rapidly. Everything seems to be going faster, and the balance points are trickier to manage.

"Louise," I said, "there are seven different areas that you can focus on in order to regain your balance when things start to teeter."

"I'm glad to hear it," she remarked. "This is all very rewarding, but it is also hard at times," she admitted. "I'll take any help I can get."

"Well," I said, "these points will help you to keep focused on the right things as you continue to learn through your company's growth."

1. Set Aside Dedicated Thinking Time

Louise, has started scheduling a minimum of a half-day per week of alone time, just to think things through, in order to stay strategic.

"When you first suggested this Michael," she commented, "I wasn't sure how I would fill a half-day every week. After doing it just twice, I realized that a half-day is probably not enough, but it is a good start. I have been coming up with really useful perspectives and strategies that support our growth plans. This time is incredibly valuable to me.

"After each of these Friday morning planning sessions that

I now have with myself, I meet with Kate and Matt to discuss what I have thought through. They have great input, which strengthens my ideas further.

"I am finding that this just makes the growth process easier. At first, I thought that this would pull me away from the more important aspects of my role. Now I know that this is probably one of the most important parts of my job."

2. Think Through the Money

The bigger the company gets, the more important it is to continue to stay clear on the fiscal aspects of the business. The most important financial statements each month are the Income Statement and the Cash Flow Forecast. Louise will need to gain an even more intimate knowledge of the company's income statement, both the current one, and the projected statement forecasting how things will evolve as the company grows.

The same is true for anticipated cash flows. By projecting the flows of cash on a month-by-month basis through this journey, issues may be anticipated and steps may be taken to deal with both issues and opportunities as they arise.

"Matt's continuing help with this makes it easy for me to handle," said Louise, "Even though he is on top of the finances, I know that I need to increase my involvement, especially when it comes to projecting our numbers through different levels of growth. Then I will know better what to expect as part of the planning process."

3. Tighten Boundaries Using Vision and Values

The bigger the game gets, the more our latitude or "wiggle room" goes away. Even small actions have large consequences. Kaizen had a client who would routinely joke around with his staff. As the company grew, even small jokes were taken out of context. He stopped being "one of the guys" and turned into this "thing" called a President.

Louise is starting to notice this already. She is being watched by her staff as they look to her for their direction.

As the company grows, Louise's continued success will be less a function of what she says "Yes" to, and more a function of what she responds to with a "No." One of her jobs moving forward will be protecting her boundaries and those of her staff. There will be many opportunities that "look good." However, if they don't fit her vision, or fit with the company's core values, it will be her job to pass on those opportunities.

Louise will need to keep clarifying, confirming, and tightening her boundaries of what is acceptable and what is not, with staff, with suppliers, and also with the company's clients. If she uses the company's vision and core values as the guideposts, she will be able to keep the company on a healthy and productive track through the different levels of growth.

"Our values have served us well so far," she commented. "I anticipate that they will continue to support us in our decision-making. They are core to our success."

4. Treat Everything as a Work in Process

Essential to further growth is to look at the company as a whole, and each department as a work in process. Louise sees three distinct elements of this. First, she sees the need to support the department managers in their respective learning curves. These people keep growing, even as their departments are doubling and tripling in size.

Yet, the principle of hiring ahead of the curve has never been more important as it is now. This is the second element of treating everything as a work in process. New staff are quickly absorbed into the workflows. Ongoing training, both at the onboarding stage and with Sponge University, is a critical element in preserving the company's quality commitment to clients.

The third area that is a work in process is the plan for process improvement and streamlining. The bigger the company gets, the more nimble it needs to be.

"We will not become a bureaucracy," stated Louise emphatically. "Our goal is to have the learning we design and build to make a meaningful difference to as many people as possible. We are much better poised to do great things if we are consistent in our delivery, yet responsive to the market. We need to continue to grow in this area."

5. Develop Metrics in Every Department

It is time for Louise and her team to develop formal measurements of the company's activities and performance in each department. With Matt and his finance team's help, she has already started this with her managers.

"We are in the process of developing dashboards of the key metrics for each department," said Louise. "These dashboards are being developed so that the managers and I can all tell whether a department is:
- handling things well;
- having troubles;
- growing and increasing the deliverables of the department;
- growing the skill-sets of the departmental staff; and
- continuing to improve and streamline its processes for implementation.

"By finding the key measures in each area, we will be able to catch issues while they are still small. This supports us to keep ourselves and all our staff growing effectively."

6. Treat Human Resources and Marketing as Strategic Resources

Human Resources – Louise is currently recruiting two more people for the HR team to ensure it is large enough to handle the recruiting needs for the next year or two. The HR department is currently focusing on the recruiting needs for the next two to four months. With the additional HR staff, they will also be able to strategize and plant the seeds for the longer-term growth in the staffing when and where it will be needed. This includes working more closely with the local colleges and universities, with industry associations, and other key strategic initiatives to locate the right people.

Once the company stabilizes its recruiting activities, the HR staff will increase their role in helping with the ongoing training and development of the company's employees at all levels.

Marketing – The goal is to staff the marketing department at a level that would reflect the company's intended size one to three years away, rather than at the current level of revenue and turnover. This is the only way that sufficient results of the marketing efforts can be achieved to ensure that Louise and her team reach their goals for growth.

In addition, Louise is treating the recruitment of staff as a marketing exercise. Emma, the marketing manager is including a focus on social media and PR to promote thought leadership of some key staff to potential staff in the market. Emma is developing a brochure for potential staff, that will be available at job fairs, recruiting events, and first interviews of candidates.

"I'm excited by what our HR and Marketing Departments can bring to help us with our plans for growth," said Louise. "Both new customers and new staff are critical for us to reach our goals."

7. Keep Growing Our Leaders

"One of the most important aspects of our growth plan," said Louise, "is to keep supporting our leadership and management team with the tools, insights, and perspectives to increase their maturity and depth. They are handling more complex challenges every day.

"They need to keep growing their skills with people, their management abilities, and their perspectives on leadership. They are already taking this on," continued Louise. "Right now, they support each other actively, and keep an eye on each other's departments. They are quick to come to the other's aid in times of stress or conflict. Yet, I know that in order to achieve what we want, they will need to keep growing."

NEXT STEPS . . .

Louise has her overall plan for this coming year already set. It will mean bringing the staffing level up significantly again, and further developing both the marketing and sales departments. She is excited by the challenges that lie ahead.

Even with an increased focus on these seven areas, Louise will still run into challenges that she doesn't expect. There will be upsets, stresses, and disappointments. There will also be accomplishments and successes and the rewards of profitable growth.

Louise knows that thinking big is essential for major growth. She also knows that thinking big is not enough. In addition to her big thinking, she has armed herself with the structures and the tools she needs to support her staff and her company, as she continues to build the business of her dreams . . .

Summary of the Seven Areas of Focus: Regaining Balance as a Company Grows

1. Set Aside Dedicated Thinking Time
2. Think Through the Money
3. Tighten Boundaries Using Vision and Values
4. Treat Everything as a Work in Process
5. Develop Metrics in Every Department
6. Treat HR and Marketing as Strategic Resources
7. Keep Growing Our Leaders

Postscript

A Letter from Louise

I received this letter by email from Louise on November 9, 2014.

Hi Michael,

Last Thursday night was a big night for us winning Elearning Development Company of the Year. Here is a link to a press article:www.trainingpressreleases.com/news/sponge/2014/sponge-uk-named-elearning-company-of-the-year

I just wanted to say an extra big thanks for all that you have done which has been instrumental in us winning this award. We have come a long way since we started working together and the award recognises and celebrates this.

At the awards ceremony, before they announced the winner, they described the company that had won, mentioning our blue chip clients and excellent customer service as well as our phenomenal growth and working with a business consultant, which impressed them. One of my abiding memories will be watching Kate's face as it slowly dawned on her that the company they were describing was us.

It's great to win awards but I am not letting this go to my head! My vision for Sponge is much bigger than the elearning awards and I look forward to working with you to realise this larger vision. But it is good to know where we stand in the marketplace benchmarked against our competitors and to be recognised for our achievements in which you have played a big part.

Thanks once again.

Louise

$\sim$

Louise requested that I add this one, last story to the book.

Michael and His Banjo

When I first met Michael at London Paddington over three years ago, I recall waiting by the Heathrow Express platform and holding his book that had his picture on the back to make sure I spotted him. He had agreed to come over to England for a few days to see if we could work together.

I was relieved when I saw someone who looked like Michael and we introduced ourselves. I then noticed that he was a carrying a big black case. So I asked him what it was. He explained to me that it was his banjo. In fact, he told me that he didn't really play it that well so he brought it along to practice. I thought to myself, who takes a flight halfway across the world carrying a banjo they don't play very well? I have to confess, at this point, I did think, "What have I done inviting over a banjo-playing Canadian? Well, if it all went pear-shaped, he could always play his banjo in his hotel room."

As readers well know, we did work together but I have often thought back to that banjo. As company owners, we all carry around our own banjos and they are our businesses. We all know what it's like when it doesn't sound right; the music is out of tune or out of time. Yet we know how we would like it to sound, a wonderful song made of complex notes that all work well together. For anyone who has played a musical instrument, in order to achieve this, regular practice is essential.

When people think about growing a business, they often miss out this piece on practice. Practicing can be tough. You need to forgive yourself when things don't always work out, keep persevering, tweaking your processes, and really celebrating when progress is made. But all the time, keeping your thoughts on the wonderful song you are learning to play. And once you've mastered that song, there is another more complex and fascinating song you want to learn just on the horizon.

So thanks, Michael, for helping us carry our banjos so the load is lighter and the music is upbeat and exciting.

Louise Pasterfield, Managing Director, Sponge UK
Elearning Development Company of the Year
Elearning Awards – 2014 Gold Winner

Afterword: Growing a Business

In this review of the journey to date of Louise Pasterfield and Sponge UK, it is clear that there are many moving parts to a business. It is also clear that there are a number of myths and misconceptions floating around that threaten to impede or halt our goals for business growth.

Louise has shared the shifts in perspective that she has gained along the way. This provides readers with useful information about the traps to avoid as we strive to achieve our goals for growth, profit, and freedom. Many people whom I have assisted and have read this story said they could resonate with what Louise went through, as they have taken a similar journey themselves.

However, there is a big difference between looking back, noticing the myths and misconceptions that have been overcome, and taking steps into the future, looking forward into the unknown. We know things will change as the future unfolds. We just don't know what or how.

I mentioned, through the dialogue with Louise in Chapter 2 that I am not a big fan of formulas. I have personally supported hundreds of people to grow their businesses since I started my consulting firm, twenty years ago. I have also worked side-by-side with other consultants, some as part of our internal team, and others in collaboration on behalf of a mutual client. In each case, the owners involved wanted to grow their particular businesses in specific ways that would serve them. Simply put, generic formulas just won't give us the level of customization needed to truly excel.

Each business is as different as each owner. We all have our own goals for ourselves, our families, our clients and customers, our employees, and for the communities in which our businesses operate. Different owners also have different strengths and varying levels of personal and business experience. These factors have a large impact on which strategies need to be employed, and how to achieve our goals for growth, profit, and freedom.

I really enjoyed Louise's description, in Chapter 2, when she said that she thought of me more like a gardener, providing what is needed, based upon the unique and individual requirements of a particular plant. What I liked about this was that different plants grow differently, even though many share the same soil. If we understand the needs of the plant, as well as the soil and weather conditions, then we can navigate our way to growing a healthy, vibrant garden with a variety of plants, all thriving within the garden.

THE CORE ISSUE

The core issue was alluded to in Chapter 1. With all the changing dynamics occurring within and around a business—those spinning plates on top of a moving foundation—we entrepreneurs just don't know how to navigate our way to significant growth to yield both more profit and more freedom.

Yet, over the past twenty years at Kaizen Consulting, we have managed to support many business owners to do just that. In fact, we do it consistently now. We have been consistently helping people achieve large-scale growth in their businesses for well over the last decade.

So, how do we do it? Is there something magic about us?

Other than the magic of being human that we all share, I am no more special than anyone else (though if she were alive, I'm sure my mom would probably disagree).

Many years ago, I was plagued with trying to figure out how to help people to get what they want. In order to accomplish this, I stumbled across a simple idea and I formed a premise. This premise is the basis of all that we have been doing in our company for the last twenty years.

THE IDEA AND A PREMISE

The idea I discovered came from my high school algebra class. There we learned first principles of mathematics. I was pretty good at math, and I enjoyed this algebra class.

The core idea of first principles is that anything can be sorted out if you break it down to its core component pieces.

Running a business has many different pieces. Yet, each piece, by itself, can be learned, understood, and addressed. That's the idea I stumbled upon. Simple, right?

From that, I formed the following premise. If I can learn, understand, address, and handle each piece (in this case, of growing a business), and if I can understand the relationship between different pieces as they work together, then eventually I can understand and handle the whole. With that understanding, I can build and grow the whole system with all its moving parts.

THREE KEYS TO SUCCESS IN GROWING A BUSINESS

If you accept my premise, then you will find these three keys most helpful:

1. Understand how each individual element of the business works, both at its most basic and fundamental level, and as it evolves and gets more complex.
2. Understand the relationships between the different components, and the dynamics of how they work together.
3. Understand the impact and consequences of change,
   a. On each of the individual elements,
   b. On the nature of the relationships, and
   c. On the business as a whole.

The Allure of and the Problem with a Formula

We want life to be simple. We don't want to have to deal with more complexity. A step-by-step formula gives us access to improving our situation. A formula also provides us with the hope that we can attain our goals easily. Let's face it. We want the easy way. Life is already too complicated. Can't we just have the step-by-step formula? We will even work it! No problem, right?

Therein lies the allure of the formula, or a step-by-step system to follow.

How can any step-by-step formula properly address all the unique elements of so many different businesses in the world? The short answer is that it cannot. Any step-by-step formula is insufficient to address the complexity. So, what do we do?

There are a number of areas that need to be addressed when growing a business. Louise and I focused on three major areas:

Structures

- Thinking through the bigger picture
- The evolving role of the owner
- Financial structures
- Operational structures

People

- Corporate culture
- Hiring
- Developing people

Sales and Marketing

- Expanding the sales process
- Building a powerful sales department
- Evolving the marketing efforts

The three areas, with their subcategories, allow us to review the main areas in the business as it grows. The one assumption I have made is that the company is already good at generating customer value at its current size. If you haven't yet mastered that, then please seek out the resources to support you in doing that first, before you grow. Otherwise, this journey is likely to turn into a disaster.

QUESTIONS VERSUS ANSWERS

We spend much of our time looking for answers. We want to know why things are the way they are, and how we can make them better. We are hungry to find the answers to the unsolved riddles in our businesses and in our lives. Yet, the real power lies in discovering better questions.

By asking more questions, we can delve deeper into situations and uncover root causes—both issues and opportunities—that often give us easier access to better solutions and better results.

Every business has areas or categories that need to be addressed to achieve growth. The categories are pretty much the same for all of us. It is the specifics within each category that vary for different entrepreneurs. If I come up with more useful questions, perhaps I can steer my company down a pathway of growth that is right for me.

QUESTIONS TO CONSIDER WHEN GROWING A BUSINESS

In order to support entrepreneurs in support of business growth, we at Kaizen Consulting have assembled a number of questions, within each of a number of different areas of a business, for readers to consider. The initial plan was to include them with this segment of the book, to give you something to consider even as you finished reading this book.

The problem is that there are so many different areas of a business, and so many different questions to consider that I couldn't find a way to do that justice, and provide something that would be useful to most readers. Further, these questions continue to be updated and are evolving all the time.

As a result, instead of trying to provide them here, in this fixed medium, we have made them available online for free. These questions are separated into different categories. Also, they have been combined with simple assessments and further guidelines for business growth. All this is available for readers of this book. On our website, you will find a series of questionnaires that have been designed to support you on your journey.

Simply go to:

www.thinkingbigisnotenough/questionsforbusinessgrowth

A COMMUNITY OF GROWTH-ORIENTED BUSINESS OWNERS

In addition to the free resources we are providing, we are developing a community of business owners worldwide who are growing a business. It is located online at www. kaizenconsulting.com/community. Feel free to come visit, hang out, share a thought or two, and learn from others on a similar journey.

One of our goals as a company is to create this community of business owners, entrepreneurs, and those interested in business growth as a place where knowledge and experiences may be shared.

Together we are stronger.
Michael Walsh

AUTHOR BIOGRAPHY

Michael Walsh is a visionary leader, speaker and author known for igniting passion in the entrepreneurs he works with by helping them drive their businesses to growth levels beyond their expectations.

In his second book he looks at practical ways to move past the traps that stop business owners from achieving their goals of growth and profit. For over twenty years, as Founder and President of Kaizen Consulting Services Inc., Michael's unique ability has been to maximize owners' goals for more profit in their business and more freedom in their lives. He also lives what he teaches: applying his methods, he has built Kaizen into a company that provides him the profit and freedom to take eighteen weeks of time off each year for personal travel, together with his family.

Walsh Business Growth Institute

Same Company - New Name.

Kaizen Consulting Services Inc. is now M. Walsh Business Growth Institute Inc.

Do you want to grow your business?

This is the same invitation Louise saw in the last book, when she decided to contact Kaizen Consulting to begin her business growth journey. We would like to extend that invitation to you.

Are you ready to take your business to the next level?

For over twenty years, Kaizen Consulting has helped entrepreneurs with businesses of all sizes to take their businesses to the next level. If you would like to explore the possibilities, please contact us:

Tel: (604) 263-5670
Email: info@kaizenconsulting.com

www.KaizenConsulting.com

Let's begin your story . . .